KU-035-380

CONTENTS

1. **Introducing the Algarve** 5
   The Land 7
   History in Brief 12
   Government and Economy 19
   The People 22

2. **In and Around Faro** 35
   Faro 36
   Along the Coast 38
   Loulé 40
   Estói and Around 42

3. **Central Algarve** 47
   Albufeira 48
   East from Albufeira 50
   West from Albufeira 52
   Inland 55
   Along the EN125 62

4. **Western Algarve** 67
   Portimão 68
   Around Portimão 70
   Lagos 72
   West along the Coast 75
   Sagres 76
   Monchique 79
   West Coast Beaches 82

5. **Eastern Algarve** 85
   Olhão 86
   Ria Formosa Nature Reserve 88
   Tavira 90
   Around Tavira 92
   On the Spanish Border 94

6. **The Alentejo** 99
   Mértola 100
   Serpa 102
   Beja 103
   Évora 105
   Discover Évora's Prehistoric Past 108
   Castles, Churches and More Dolmens 110
   Évora-Monte 112
   Estremoz 112
   Vila Viçosa 116
   South to Monsaraz 118

Travel Tips 122

Index 127

1
Introducing the Algarve

The Algarve is Portugal's playground. In terms of land area it covers no more than an eighth of the country but nevertheless has more hotel rooms, holiday apartments and villas for rent than the rest of **Portugal** put together. The key attraction for most of the three million or so European tourists who holiday in the Algarve each year is its pleasant climate. **Sunshine** is virtually guaranteed for six months of the year, while spring comes early and even in the depths of winter afternoon temperatures usually reach a pleasant 15°C (59°F).

With more than 30 top-class **golf courses**, numerous tennis and riding centres, and facilities for just about every water sport under the sun, the Algarve is a popular choice for active holiday-makers. More indolent travellers are drawn by the marvellous **beaches** which, as well as the weather, are among the best in Europe. Washed by Atlantic water and sheltered by honey-coloured sandstone cliffs west of Faro, they extend along almost the entire southern coast. In the far west are mile after mile of magnificent beaches, where those seeking solitude and the simple life can escape the crowds. East of Faro the distinctive landscape of sand bars, lagoons and offshore beaches, now part of the **Ria Formosa Nature Reserve**, is well worth exploration.

The water of the Atlantic is much cooler than that of the Mediterranean, and even in summer it may be a little chilly for those accustomed to warmer seas. It is at its warmest in the sheltered lagoons which extend along the eastern part of the province.

TOP ATTRACTIONS

*** **Silves:** see the atmospheric castle of Silves.
*** **Lagos:** the history and style of this fascinating city.
*** **Western Algarve:** explore the wild coastline.
*** **The Alentejo:** visit the medieval frontier fortresses.
*** **Évora:** its amazing concentration of beautiful historic buildings.
** **Northern Algarve:** the lushly wooded hills of this wonderful region.
** **Barrier Islands:** a boat trip to these islands east of Faro.

Opposite: *Golf is one of the many sports enjoyed in the Algarve. Magnificent views add to the attraction.*

Above: *Traditional tiles demonstrate the Algarve's Moorish heritage.*
Below: *The Algarve is famous for its beaches – this lovely example is Praia do Pinhão, near Lagos.*

The Algarve is a place where you can take it easy. There are no hidden hassles or pitfalls for the unwary traveller. Just relax and enjoy the sunshine, try the delightful and inexpensive local wines, dine out on what is arguably the best **seafood** in Europe, and enjoy the good-natured company of your Portuguese hosts.

Many holiday-makers never stir beyond their comfortable sun loungers. But those that do make the effort discover a fascinating hinterland of hills and forests, villages and farms, castles and churches. And there is plenty of history associated with the coast itself. Many seaside towns have witnessed the comings and goings of generations of traders and empire builders, from the Phoenicians, Carthaginians and Romans onwards.

However, it was the Moors who left their mark most indelibly during an occupation which lasted over 500 years. The name Algarve derives from *al-Gharb* – Arabic for the Western Lands – and Moorish influence can still be seen today in everything from decorative tiles to contemporary building styles.

The great plains of the **Alentejo** to the north are, as yet, little known outside Portugal, but the province is one of the most distinctive and fascinating regions of Western Europe. The Alentejo is a land of wide horizons, atmospheric medieval castles, and vast agricultural estates whose divisions date back to Roman times. Here the ancient city of **Évora** has been designated a UNESCO World Heritage Site by virtue of its wealth of historic monuments.

One common factor of any holiday in the Algarve or Alentejo is the friendliness and hospitality of the local people. Tourism may have replaced agriculture and fishing as the leading industry on the coast, but visitors to the area still receive a warm and distinctively Portuguese welcome.

THE LAND

The Algarve is a distinctive province physically as well as culturally. Bordered on the west and south by the **Atlantic**, it is divided from the rest of Portugal by a series of low mountain ranges which reach their highest elevation of 902m (2960ft) at **Foia**. In the extreme east the **Guadiana River** forms the border with Spain. From east to west the province is about 155km (95 miles) long and around 50km (30 miles) wide.

The schists and shales of the northern hills make for poor acid soils, and the landscape varies between moorland of heathers, gorse, broom and cistus (rock rose), and woods of chestnut, oak, beech and pine in the valleys. Eucalyptus trees have been introduced to provide pulp for the paper industry – a controversial decision according to naturalists, as they siphon off a great deal of water and do not provide the right habitat for native insects, birds and animals.

Above: *Mixed deciduous woods flourish in river valleys, in this case at Fonte de Benemola.*

Immediately south is the **Barrocal**, a lens-shaped strip of limestone which sweeps from **Cabo de São Vicente** (Cape St Vincent) in the west to **Tavira**. It reaches its widest point of 20km (12½ miles) in the central Algarve.

Here you find maquis, the typical southern European scrub vegetation, known in Portugal as *matos*. Holly oak, wild olive, cistus and other shrubs grow here alongside rosemary, lavender, thyme, sage and wild flowers. The valleys between the ridges have rich red soils and provide fertile farmland. Carob, almond, orange, lemon and fig trees – all introduced by the Moors – thrive here.

The western half of the coastal Algarve is dominated by sandstone, quarried to produce the red rock you can still see in the walls of ruined castles. Sandstone is also responsible for the distinctive ochre-coloured cliffs which have been weathered into stacks, grottoes, caves and coves.

Below: *Cork oak bark, dried before processing, is a common sight in the northern Algarve during summer.*

East of Faro the low-lying coastal flats are one of the most important **wetland** areas in western Europe and provide habitat for resident and migrating birds. The salt marsh vegetation here may not be pretty but it supplies a great deal of nutrients and shelter for birds, fish, molluscs and crustaceans. A string of barrier islands separates the in-shore lagoon from the sea, and dune vegetation such as marram grass, thrift and cotton weed help to anchor the shifting sands.

The Alentejo consists of rolling plains with a few small ranges of hills; the **Serra d'Ossa** south of Estremoz rises to 653m (2142ft). Arable **farming** is the most common land use, but there are also large tracts of heathland which provide grazing for sheep, cattle and pigs as well as cork oak forests. The region has been severely affected by drought since 1990.

The Algarve gets more rainfall and also has extensive underground sources, but the local government in Faro is becoming concerned about maintaining water stocks. The profligate use of water to maintain golf courses in particular has come under close scrutiny, and golf clubs may be forced to used recycled water in the future.

Climate

The Algarve has a **mild** climate, with little rainfall and plenty of sunny days, which is why the area is so popular with outdoor sports enthusiasts and those seeking year-round sunshine. Sea temperatures are on average lower than the Mediterranean, despite being warmed by the **Gulf Stream**, and are cooler the further west you go.

Both the Algarve and Alentejo receive most of their rain in winter. Rain is rare between June and September, but you can expect wet weather lasting four days or more any time between November and April. Spring starts early, marked by a profusion of colourful wild flowers and is probably the best time to visit, before the temperatures soar and the hordes of tourists arrive. Summers are **hot** and **sunny** but are refreshed by cooling breezes on the coast; the further west you go the windier it gets. July and August are the hottest months, and the landscape becomes parched and barren. Autumn and winter days are **mild**, but you will need a jacket in the evening and some kind of heating in your apartment or hotel room. January is the **coolest** month.

Above: *Traditional wells, or* nora, *eke out ground water during the long summers in rural areas.*

ALMOND BLOSSOM

The almond tree was brought to the Algarve by the Moors, and its delightful white blossoms cover the countryside in February. It was introduced, so the legend goes, by a Moorish king who wished to please his Scandinavian bride who was pining for the snows of her native land. He planted the countryside around his castle with almond trees so that once a year she would feel at home, surrounded by drifts of snowy white blossom.

COMPARATIVE CLIMATE CHART	FARO				PRAIA DA ROCHA				VILA REAL DE S. ANTONIO			
	WIN JAN	SPR APR	SUM JUL	AUT OCT	WIN JAN	SPR APR	SUM JUL	AUT OCT	WIN JAN	SPR APR	SUM JUL	AUT OCT
MAX TEMP. °C	17	23	28	20	16	22	27	19	18	24	30	20
MIN TEMP. °C	8	13	18	11	9	13	18	11	7	13	17	10
MAX TEMP. °F	63	73	83	68	61	71	81	66	63	75	85	68
MIN TEMP. °F	47	55	64	52	48	56	64	53	45	55	63	50
RAINFALL mm	63	22	6	82	55	23	6	65	61	26	5	72
RAINFALL in	2.2	0.6	0.2	2.7	2.3	0.8	0.2	2.7	2.3	1	0.2	2.7

Above: *Spring flowers carpet the countryside.*
Below: *The mild climate ensures that subtropical and Mediterranean flowers bloom throughout the year.*

Plant Life

Between February and June the landscape is transformed into a blaze of colour by thousands of species of wild flowers. These burst into life everywhere – on the sand dunes and cliffs, the rocky hills and roadside verges. Yellow is the predominant colour in February when mimosa, celandine and bermuda buttercups bloom beneath the pink and white almond blossom. In March it's the turn of pink, blue and scarlet pimpernels, irises and rock roses. In late spring look out for oleander, gladioli, tulips, orchids and jacarandas.

The wonderful wild flower displays are aided by the traditional farming methods in the hilly interior. Pesticides are not yet used in great quantities and many of the practices you can still see today, such as hay being reaped by hand, mule and donkey-drawn carts and the yearly rotation of vegetable plots, have not changed since medieval times. The land looks well cared for and respected, but the same cannot be said of the wildlife.

Wildlife

Of the larger birds, storks are common, and build their nests on bell towers and other high buildings. Flamingoes can be seen at **Castro Marim** during the winter. Eagles, kites, owls and Egyptian vultures are also occasionally seen. **Cabo de São Vicente** is an important staging post for migrating birds during autumn and spring. The **Ria Formosa Nature Reserve** is the best place to see wading birds, such as the long-legged black-winged stilts, and ducks. Migrating sea birds can be seen off the west coast in large numbers during spring and autumn. Cattle egrets are common in the **Alentejo**, while two of the most exotic birds are bee-eaters and hoopoes.

Land mammals are few and far between. Rabbits and hares are hunted for food; there are a few foxes, badgers, genets and Egyptian mongooses. In the southern Alentejo deer, now vanished, were once common, as were lynx and wolves. Of the larger animals which once roamed freely only wild boar remain.

Bird and mammal numbers are declining because of lack of protection and unrestricted hunting. Hunters will shoot anything that moves; something walkers should bear in mind between August and March. Their target is as likely to be tiny songbirds, stray cats and rare species as game.

The only mildly venomous snake is the viper which is found in the mountains; you are more likely to see the (non-poisonous) horseshoe snake. Geckoes are much more common and you may even be lucky enough to see a chameleon, green lizard, terrapin or salamander. The most bothersome insect is the mosquito.

SHEEPDOG

When in the Alentejo, you may be lucky enough to spot a huge white sheepdog standing over a metre (40in) at the shoulder. This is the **Rafeiro Alentejano**, bred to protect the flocks from wolves. The lightweight Iberian wolf (now vanished from the Alentejo) would have been completely intimidated by such a powerful adversary. There are very few examples of the breed left, as many were killed by farm workers following the 1974 revolution in order to allow easy access to livestock. However, a breeding society has now been set up; if you're in **Évora** at the end of June you'll be able to catch the annual **Rafeiro Show**.

Below: *Tall buildings in quiet surroundings are ideal for storks. The pair return to the same nest every spring.*

HISTORY IN BRIEF
Birth of a Nation 7000BC to AD1000

Portugal has been inhabited since at least 7000BC, and had built up a Neolithic castroculture, based on hilltop forts, by 1000BC. **Celts** moved to the Iberian peninsula around 700BC, about the same time trading **Phoenicians** and **Greeks** were visiting the Algarve.

Carthaginians, from what is now Tunisia, controlled the Algarve from around 535BC, but the Iberian peninsula passed from their hands to the Romans after the Second Punic War in 202BC. The legions met strong resistance from the Lusitanians, a tribe based in central Portugal whose leader, Viriatus, is a celebrated figure in Portuguese folklore. It was not until Julius Caesar established permanent colonies in Évora, Beja, Mértola and Lisbon around 60BC that Portugal finally became integrated into the **Roman Empire**. Portugal can still trace its Roman antecedents in its language, roads, legal system and *latifúndios* – huge agricultural estates that still survive in parts of the Alentejo.

After the fall of the Roman Empire the power vacuum was eventually filled by the Visigoths, Romanized Christians from eastern France and Germany. An elite warrior caste with a base in Faro, they were never numerous enough to make their mark on Portugal. In AD711 **Moors** from North Africa crossed the straits of Gibraltar. They met with little resistance from the local people, who had become alienated from their rulers through weak government and religious persecution, and within a decade the Moors had conquered vast tracts of the Iberian peninsula.

Most Moors were Berbers from Morocco, but Egyptians settled in

Below: *The Roman ruins at Milreu near Faro are the most extensive in the Algarve and date from the 1st century AD.*

HISTORICAL CALENDAR

c. 2000BC Neolithic settlements in hill forts.
c. 1000BC Phoenicians from Middle East develop trading posts in the Algarve.
210BC Romans occupy the Algarve and Alentejo.
AD415 Visigoths take over the Iberian peninsula.
711 Berbers from North Africa and Arabs invade and conquer Iberia within seven years.
1143 Afonso Henriques recognized as first king of Portucale after victories against the Moors.
1249 Afonso III completes reconquest of the Algarve.
1385 Invading Castilian army beaten at battle of Aljubarrota; start of the Avis dynasty.
1418 Henry the Navigator becomes governor of the Algarve and initiates voyages of discovery.
1498 Vasco da Gama reaches India.
1580 Portugal annexed by Spain following end of the Avis dynasty.
1640 Independence restored; Braganças invited to rule.
1755 Massive earthquake destroys towns throughout southern Portugal.
1807 Napoleon invades Portugal but is driven out five years later.
1832–4 War of the Two Brothers resulting in a new and more liberal constitution.
1908 Republicans assassinate King Carlos I in Lisbon.
1910 End of monarchy; Portugal becomes a republic.
1932–68 Salazar dictatorship.
1974 Revolution followed by the drafting of a new democratic constitution and freedom for overseas colonies.
1986 Portugal joins the European Community.

the area between Beja and Faro, and Yemenites from the Arabian peninsula turned Silves into the regional capital. At its peak **Silves** was likened to Baghdad, and was a city of opulent architecture and scholarship at a time when the rest of Europe was languishing in the Dark Ages. The Moors were tolerant and civilized, and this was a stable and prosperous time for the people of southern Portugal. Agricultural methods improved and new crops such as oranges, lemons, almonds, cotton and rice were introduced.

Christian Reconquest and Consolidation 1000–1400

By the 11th century Christian forces had won back parts of northern Portugal, an area between the Douro and Minho rivers which was known as Portucale. Over the next century central Portugal passed into Christian hands with the aid of **Crusader** armies from northern Europe, but the **Moors** managed to retain the Alentejo and Algarve. As the land was reconquered, territory was granted to those able to defend it, enabling the Church, the **Knights Templar** and many nobles to gain enormous power.

CAROB

Carob is a high-protein animal food and was the 'locust' which John the Baptist ate in the Bible. The pods look like pea pods, hanging from the tall evergreen carob tree. Known as *kirat* in Arabic, the weight of the carob bean sets the standard for the carat, which is still used as a measure for diamonds and other precious stones.

CARAVEL

The Great Discoveries were made possible by the invention of a revolutionary new sailing ship. The caravel's triangular sails, adapted from Arab dhows, made it possible to sail into the wind. Earlier sailing ships had only one mast and a square rig. The caravel was a lightweight and manoeuvrable vessel with three sails. Later models added a topsail and square sail for running before the wind.

Afonso Henriques was calling himself King of Portugal by the mid-12th century, but he and his successors had great difficulty trying to dislodge the Moors from the south. Faro and the Western Algarve did not fall until 1249. The Algarve's separate status is underlined by the titles of the early rulers, who were styled King of Portugal and the Algarve.

The principal threat to the new kingdom of Portugal was now the rising power of Castile in Spain. **Dom Dinis** (1279–1325) built no less than 50 fortresses along the Spanish border to protect the kingdom; many of these can be seen today in the Alentejo. Known as El Rei Lavrador, the farmer king, he introduced agricultural reforms, revitalized the mining industry and expanded maritime trade.

After peace was finally agreed with Castile following a decisive Portuguese victory in 1385, the kingdom was free to turn its attention further afield. Given Portugal's strategic location between the Atlantic and the Mediterranean, it was inevitable that maritime expansion would follow. The map of the world would never be the same again.

The Great Discoveries

It was the Portuguese who mapped the world as we know it, and they established a trading empire which encompassed Brazil, Macau, India and Africa. The early navigators were the astronauts of their day, and the Algarve was the launchpad for their voyages.

They were the first Europeans to cross the **equator**, round the **Cape of Good Hope** and reach **India** by sea. They 'discovered' **South America**, landed in **Australia** 200 years before Captain Cook, and were the first to trade with **China** and **Japan**.

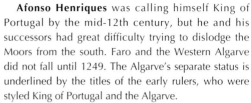

INFANTE
D HENRIQUE

V CENTENARIO DA SUA MORTE
1460 · 1960

Left: *This bust of Vasco da Gama in the gardens of Estói Palace commemorates one of the world's greatest explorers. He pioneered the sea route to India via the Cape of Good Hope.*
Opposite: *Henry the Navigator changed the map of the world. This statue is in Lagos.*

The Portuguese were almost certainly in North America years before Christopher Columbus. Mariners from the Atlantic islands of the **Azores** (themselves only discovered in 1427) were fishing the Grand Banks off **Newfoundland** some 40 years before Columbus's epic voyage of discovery. However, many who sailed west did not return. 'God gave the Portuguese a small country as their cradle but all the world as their grave,' was how the 17th-century Jesuit writer **Padre António Vieira** described the common fate of early explorers.

The driving force behind the great voyages of discovery was **Prince Henry the Navigator**. Born in 1394, the third son of King João I and an English noblewoman, Philippa of Lancaster, he became governor of the Algarve, moved to Lagos and founded a school of navigation. Whether this was actually situated west along the coast at Sagres, and whether the great compass rose which can be seen there really dates from the 15th century, is open to conjecture. But certainly the Sagres promontory which marks the far southwestern tip of Europe – and which at the time marked the end of the known world – has become as inexorably linked with the Great Discoveries as Cape Canaveral has with the exploration of space.

DOM SEBASTIÃO AND ALCÁCER-QUIBIR

Historians debate whether **Dom Sebastião** (1557–1578) was a foolish young man or completely mad. He was driven by an obsession to exterminate Muslims, and accordingly set sail for Africa with a fleet of 500 warships in 1578. Here his forces, suffering from heat exhaustion and lack of water, were no match for the Muslim defenders on their home ground. Only a few hundred out of the 23,000-strong force escaped slaughter or capture at the Battle of **Alcácer-Quibir**. Most of the Portuguese nobility perished, along with Sebastião. As he left no heir, Portugal was annexed by Spain. But many believed Sebastião had not died and would come back to make Portugal great again.

TEA WITH THE QUEEN

Afternoon tea is such an ingrained part of the English tradition that it comes as a surprise to hear that it was a Portuguese princess who popularized the ceremony. Tea became a fashionable drink in Portugal in the 17th century, and **Catherine of Bragança** imported the custom to England when she married King Charles II in 1662. Her dowry included **Tangier** and **Bombay**. Tea drinking caught on in England but was largely abandoned in Portugal in favour of coffee.

Below: *The revolt of 1640 ended 60 years of Spanish rule. The scene is captured in the tiled back to a park bench in Portimão.*

In 1419, one of Henry's ships returned to the Algarve with the news of a small uninhabited island 643km (400 miles) to the southwest. This was Porto Santo; a year later its sister island Madeira was discovered. Henry colonized the fertile volcanic island with farmers from the Algarve, shipping in vines from Crete and sugar cane, cattle, wheat and barley.

By the middle of the century the west coast of Africa had been opened up for trade; caravels laden with gold, slaves and ivory returned to Lagos and financed future expeditions. **Bartolomeu Dias** rounded the Cape of Good Hope in 1488; **Vasco da Gama** finally reached India in 1498 and Brazil was claimed for Portugal two years later.

Age of Empire 1500–1900

In the 16th century Portugal was the richest nation on earth, with trading posts in Goa, Malacca, Ceylon and Macau as well as along the African coast. Gold, ivory, spices, silks and silver flooded into the country. The reign of **Manuel I** (1495–1521) was Portugal's **Golden Age**, but the wealth remained in the hands of the usual beneficiaries: the Crown, the Church and the aristocracy. With a population of one and a half million, Portugal did not have the human resources to consolidate its trading empire.

The **Inquisition**, imported from Spain but embraced enthusiastically by the Portuguese, meant that knowledge was controlled by the Church. The great flowering of ideas promised by the European Renaissance was strangled at birth in Portugal. Thousands were tortured for straying from religious orthodoxy, and in 1496 the Jews were expelled from the peninsula. This deprived Portugal of much commercial expertise and the economy began to decline. The rule of the increasingly decadent **House of Avis** ended

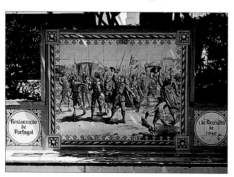

with the death of the heirless **Sebastião** on a Moroccan battlefield in 1578. Spain then seized the crown.

Sixty years of **Spanish** rule gained Portugal the enmity of her oldest ally, England – the Spanish armada which sailed to attack England in 1588 left from Lisbon – and the Dutch, losing the country vital trade which was never fully recovered. In 1640 a popular revolt deposed the Spanish governor and put the Portuguese nobleman, the **Duke of Bragança**, on the throne.

The discovery of gold and diamonds in Brazil during the late 17th century sparked off a mass emigration and helped Portugal to rebuild its economy. The **Great Earthquake** of 1755 threw the nation into crisis but allowed the king's chief minister, the **Marquês de Pombal**, to push through some much-needed reforms.

Pombal was one of Portugal's most dynamic figures. He introduced state schools, set up export companies to promote the tobacco, whaling, fishing and port industries, abolished slavery in Portugal, attempted to end discrimination by colour and religion, expelled the Jesuits and curtailed the power of the Inquisition. Pombal's methods included the torture and imprisonment of enemies and he ended his days in disgrace, but his liberal reforms survived him.

Above: *The Marquês de Pombal – iconoclast, liberal reformer and ruthless despot.*

EARTHQUAKE

1 November 1755 is a date every Portuguese schoolchild knows by heart. It was **All Saints Day** and most people were at mass when the **Great Earthquake** struck, destroying almost every church in southern Portugal along with their worshippers inside. In Lisbon 17,000 out of 20,000 houses were razed to the ground. Faro, Tavira and Lagos were all devastated by the shocks and the aftermath of landslides, tidal waves and fires. At least 60,000 were killed in the worst earthquake ever recorded in Europe.

Napoleon's troops invaded Portugal in 1807 and the monarchy fled to Brazil. Under British leadership Portugal forced the French to withdraw to Spain five years later. A group of Portuguese army officers demanded a new and more liberal constitution which included universal male suffrage and a curtailment of aristocratic and church privileges. **King João VI** accepted the terms and returned from Brazil in 1821, but his younger son, **Miguel**, led a reactionary counter movement against the crown prince, **Pedro**. This was the **War of the Two Brothers**, which ended in 1834 after Spain, France and Britain took the liberal side. The rest of the 19th century witnessed almost constant struggle between those who wanted liberal reforms and those who did not, and was a time of ineffective foreign policy and declining living standards.

Portugal in the 20th Century

The army and urban poor, disenchanted by government ineptitude, turned to Republicanism. In 1908 the king and his eldest son were assassinated, and in 1910 the monarchy was finally overthrown by an army coup. A series of short-lived parliaments and military intervention came to an end in 1932 when **Dr António Salazar**, a university economics lecturer, became prime minister, a post he held until 1968. Salazar managed to improve and modernize the economy, but at the expense of democracy. A fascist dictator in all but name, he was a great friend of Spain's General Franco and admired Hitler, though Portugal remained neutral in World War II. Salazar's successor, **Marcelo Caetano**, promised more democracy, but continued to wage deeply unpopular colonial wars in Africa.

Discontent in the African-based army crystallized into hardline opposition. In 1974, in a bloodless left-wing revolution, the army took over and were joined by socialists of all persuasions amid a mood of euphoric liberation and rejoicing. Provisional governments came and went, and there were periods of virtual anarchy, but the colonies gained independence and the November

1975 elections gave the **Socialist Party** an impressive victory. Portugal was finally free from the whims of kings, despots, generals, cardinals and dictators, and the country's fortunes were at last in the hands of its people.

GOVERNMENT AND ECONOMY

Government and Politics

Portugal is a multiparty democracy with parliamentary deputies elected by proportional representation every four years. The centre-right PSD, or Social Democrats, whose free market policies were popular in the boom years of the 1980s, were defeated in 1995 by the Socialist party led by Antonio Guterres. Elected on an anti-corruption and pro-education platform, the Socialists' economic policies and pro-European stance did not differ much from those of their predecessors. In 2002 Portugal returned the Social Democrats to power again, but with a narrow majority. Weak and increasingly unpopular, the government was forced to call early elections. The current prime minister is **José Socrates**, the PS (Socialist) leader, who was elected in 2005. Anibal Cavaco Silva, the former PSD prime minister, was elected president in 2006. There are three tiers of government below the national level: regional, municipal and parish. The seat of local government in the Algarve is Faro.

Economic Development

Portugal has languishied at or near the bottom of the European Union wealth table since joining in 1986. It currently has a lower GDP per head than newer members Slovenia, Malta and Cyprus. It is an enthusiastic

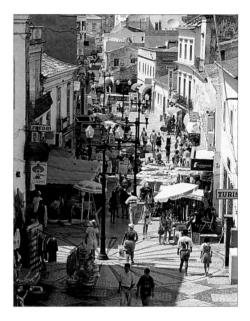

Above: *A bustling street scene in Albufeira, the largest resort in the Algarve.*

TOURISM

Tourism accounts for 7% of Portugal's GDP, one of the highest ratios in the EU. It employs 500,000 people (11% of the active population) and nets $16 billion annually. In the Algarve tourism accounts for 45% of regional employment and almost half of the bed-nights spent by foreigners in Portuguese hotels.

The most important crops produced in the Algarve for centuries were almonds, carob, cork oaks, figs, grapes and olives. Commercially grown oranges, lemons and grapefruit are now supplanting these traditional crops, as production is less labour intensive and demand high. But you can still see plenty of evidence of the former mainstays of the economy.

Above: *Despite increasing modernization, many small boats still use traditional fishing methods.*
Below: *Harnessing the power of the Atlantic breezes in the windy western Algarve.*

member of the Union and the grateful recipient of grants to modernize infrastructure and industry. The road system in particular, which was formerly one of the worst in Europe, has been extensively improved.

Clothing and shoe making are strong areas in the manufacturing sector; industries such as steel, car manufacture, light engineering and cement are concentrated in the northern part of the country. Portugal's main trading partners are Spain, Germany, France, the UK and Italy.

Agriculture

The agricultural industry, characterized by low productivity and outdated methods, cannot compete with countries with intensive farming methods such as Spain. At present it is cheaper for Portugal to import wheat. The Algarve is currently modernizing its **fishing** industry with computerized plants and less labour intensive factories.

Many of the wealthy families who fled to Brazil, Spain and France after the 1974 revolution have now returned and are again living in style. The gap in earnings between rich and poor, which fell after 1974, is rising again with the growth of the middle classes. However, two-thirds of the population remains rural rather than urban.

While Portugal ranks in the top third of the world in terms of GNP, life expectancy and infant mortality, it barely scrapes into the top half in terms of literacy and education. A 1989 study revealed that 21% of the population was illiterate, many being elderly country women who had never received formal education under the Salazar dictatorship.

Tourism

In the Algarve tourism is by far the leading industry and accounts for over 50% of earnings. The province's population quadruples every August as visitors pour in by air, rail and road; the majority are Spanish with the UK, Germany and France next in line. Tourism really only got under way with the opening of Faro airport in 1965. Growth was briefly halted by the revolution of 1974; the second half of the 1970s saw major developments take shape.

With planning controls implemented by Salazar gone, the building boom gathered momentum, reaching its peak in the get-rich-quick days of the mid-1980s. Things have improved substantially since then. Local councils have improved amenities in many resorts. Many have been landscaped and roads have been improved with the help of European Community money. Furthermore, developers, forced to confront the issue of rentability, have lost interest in churning out yet another apartment block.

Further construction work has been halted by new legislation. Land use has been redefined; in some areas building is completely forbidden and in others, such as the coastline of the western Algarve, only small scale developments will be permitted. Critics say it's a case of too little, too late. But, although mistakes have been made, it's impossible to turn the clock back and at least an effort is being made to safeguard the future.

MARKET DAYS

Local markets are fun, and sell a variety of goods. Local tourist offices can give details of the locations.
Albufeira: First and third Tuesday of each month.
Alte: Third Thursday of each month.
Alvor: Second Tuesday of each month.
Estói: Second Sunday of each month.
Lagos: First Saturday of each month.
Loulé: Saturday mornings.
Monchique: Second Friday of each month.
Paderne: First Saturday of each month.
Portimão: First Monday of each month.
Quarteira: Every Wednesday.
Silves: Third Monday of each month.
Tavira: Third Monday of each month.

Below: *Terracotta and ceramic pottery with traditional designs make eye-catching souvenirs.*

Above: *Country children work alongside their parents in the fields from an early age.*

North of the EN125, tourism has made little impact. Rather than build new holiday accommodation, locals are given financial incentives to restore old houses and offer rooms to visitors. There are plenty of places to stay with a distinctive Portuguese feel if you look beyond the major resorts.

THE PEOPLE

Dealing with different cultures has been part of the Algarve way of life for millennia. As a consequence the local people have a tolerant and relaxed attitude to visitors. More laid-back and less macho than their Spanish neighbours, and less serious than the northern Portuguese, they are friendly and hospitable.

They do, however, have a southern attitude to time keeping – urgency is an alien concept, and it's best to be flexible should you need someone's help in getting a problem solved. The matter will be sorted out eventually, but the delay can be frustrating for those still locked into northern time.

The Portuguese have a deeply ambiguous attitude to Spain. 'Only ill winds and bad marriages come from Spain' is how the medieval proverb goes, and there is still a certain amount of distrust. On the one hand they have more in common culturally with Spain than with their other partners in the European Union, and have close financial and economic ties with their larger and more prosperous neighbour. On the other, they fear loss of independence – not politically as 500 years ago, but in terms of the global financial market. Spaniards are widely regarded as arrogant and overbearing, and their superior buying power (wages can be 30% above the Portuguese average) is envied.

One characteristic trait of the Portuguese, which has no exact English equivalent, is *saudade*. This can best be described as a mood of bittersweet sadness, a nostalgia for a lost Golden Age which harks back to the time when Portugal ruled the seas.

Language

The **Portuguese** language is heavily derived from **Latin**. If you already speak Spanish, French or Italian, you'll be able to understand some words when you come across the written language – most menus, road signs and museum information will be in Portuguese. However, the nasal sounds and heavy inflection make spoken Portuguese hard to pronounce or understand. If in difficulty and looking for an English speaker, you should approach a younger person as they are more likely to have learned English in school. English is widely spoken in tourist areas; however, the Portuguese appreciate efforts to speak their language and are tolerant of mistakes, so have a go!

Religion

While the vast majority of Portuguese are nominally **Catholic**, the south has always been less religious than the north. The Alentejo in particular has a strong tradition of **anti-clericalism**, which dates back to the times when vast tracts of land were owned by the church. Agricultural workers were (and many are still) extremely poor, and it's not surprising that the Alentejo was and is one of the strongholds of the Communist Party. Most churchgoers are elderly and many churches are permanently locked up for lack of custom. Anglican services are held in some resorts.

PRONUNCIATION

When the tilde accent (~) is placed over *ao* (as in Portimão) it creates an *ow* sound with just the hint of *oo* to follow. An *m* at the end of words is sounded like a combination of *m* and *n*; '*bom*' (good) sounds almost like '*bong*,' but the *g* is only a faint whisper. The letter *s* at the end of a word or before a consonant is pronounced *sh*; *x* also makes a *sh* sound. The letter *c* is soft before *e* and *i*, hard otherwise unless it has a cedilla attached. The combination *nh* sounds like the *ny* of canyon; *lh* is pronounced *ly*. Good luck!

Below: *Only the elderly are regular churchgoers these days.*

February Variable date just before Lent. Carnival, Loulé.

March or April Easter Sunday. Procession of Mãe Soberana, Loulé.

25 April National Holiday to celebrate the start of the 1974 revolution.

Last week in April Agricultural and Handicrafts Fair, Estremoz.

May Day Celebrations and folk festivals throughout Algarve.

1–3 May Festival of the Pine, held in Estói.

30–31 May Country Fair, Vila Viçosa.

June World Music Festival, Loulé.

10 June National Holiday to celebrate poet Camões.

13 June Feast of Santo António, Reguengos.

24, 25, 26 June Feast of São João (John the Baptist), Évora.

Late June Beer Festival, Silves.

16 July Feira da Nossa Senhora do Carmo, Faro.

July/August International Jazz Festival, Loulé.

August Olhão's famous Seafood Festival; Country Fair, Lagoa; Folk Festival, Tavira.

15 August Feast of the Assumption, Castro Marim.

August/September Medieval days, Castro Marim.

September Algarve Folk Music and Dance Festival.

26–28 September Country Fair, Viana do Alentejo.

10 October National Holiday to celebrate the founding of the republic in 1910; and Feast of Santa Iria, Faro.

26–28 October Country Fair, held in Monchique.

1 November All Saints Day (National Holiday).

25 December Christmas Day.

• The Algarve Tourist Board produces a free monthly calendar of events.

Traditional Culture

Music: Portuguese *saudade* reaches its fullest expression, on a personal level, in *fado* music, where the performers sing hauntingly of fate, lost love and broken dreams to a guitar accompaniment. It is an emotional experience rather than entertainment and the audience is held spellbound. More common in Lisbon and northern Portugal than the south, you may nevertheless be lucky enough to catch a performance in the Algarve.

One thing you will certainly hear are sinuous **Brazilian** and **African** rhythms. Thousands of Africans from Mozambique and Angola fled to Portugal to escape the devastating civil wars which were a legacy of colonialism. On a sultry night with stars gleaming above the palm trees, these vibrant tropical sounds add to the exotic flavour.

Festivals: The Algarve reflects the Portuguese passion for holidays and festivals – hardly a week goes by without some local celebration. Festivals may be religious (*romarias*) or secular (*festas*), but they are all exuberant affairs celebrated with parades, fireworks and plenty of song and dance. Events in smaller villages will probably be less touristy and more fun.

Folk dancing is still popular in Portugal, and you should be able to see dancers at the local festivals, or in some of the hotels or specific folk dancing venues. The most common dance is the *corridinho*, an exuberant whirling, foot stamping jig.

Sport and Recreation
Golf
In and Around Faro

Quinta do Lago: Within this estate are four excellent courses. **San Lorenzo**, which forms part of the Ria Formosa Nature Reserve, is a combination of testing golf and wonderful scenery. Designed by Joseph Lee, its 18 widely varying holes run past pine trees, beaches and lagoons, the latter forming natural water hazards. Many regard it as the most beautiful course in Portugal – it's certainly one of the most challenging. Almost every hole on the **Quinta do Lago North** course, adjoining the Ria Formosa Nature Reserve, involves some kind of dogleg and demands an accurate drive. **Quinta do Lago South** is regarded as one of the greatest golf courses in the world. Based on sandy soil covered with pines, broom, heather and wild flowers, it is testing and provides a real challenge for players with a higher handicap. The Portuguese Open has been held here several times. The first nine at

Above: *The look of concentration on these young dancers' faces as they await their cue says it all.*
Opposite: *Folk dancing is still a living tradition in the Algarve; the village of Alte stages regular performances.*

MEDIA

English-language newspapers and magazines are aimed mostly at the expat community. The main ones are the weekly *Anglo-Portuguese News* and the fortnightly *Algarve News*. *Discover* magazine has lists of forthcoming local events, nightlife and festivals, and is available from tourist offices and some large hotels. You'll find foreign newspapers are available at most of the major towns and resorts.

Pinheiros Altos is carved out of a pine forest and the second is built around lakes and sand traps. The short par fours are deceptive, and the lake beds are full of stray balls. Designed by Ronald Fream, the course is used by professionals for pre-season practice. There's an adjoining golf academy with automatic video replay and multi-lingual instructors.

Above: *Hole Number Six at Quinta do Lago.*

Vale do Lobo: Formerly three sets of nine holes, this world-famous course now consists of the 18-hole Royal Course, partly designed by Henry Cotton, and two nine-hole loops comprising the less challenging Ocean course. Hole 16 on the Royal requires a 218m (715ft) shot over cliffs to achieve a par three. Golfers enjoy spectacular sea views, and the rolling fairways run over sandy ground past eucalyptus, pine, olive and orange trees. Most of the holes are designed for pleasure rather than punishment – true holiday golf.

Central Algarve

Vila Sol: This course, just 4km (2½ miles) north of Vilamoura, has hosted the Portuguese Open twice. The land is ideal for golf; sandy and fast-draining with umbrella pines, fig and almond trees, and cork oaks dotted around the course. English architect Donald Steel has laid out a challenging course where the narrow fairways demand accuracy. The first four holes are the most difficult (tel: 289 300 505). Also close to Vilamoura is the **Victoria Course**, opened in 2004 and the longest 18-hole course in Portugal. It has the potential to host major competitions (tel: 289 320 500).

Vilamoura: There are now four courses in this ever-growing resort. The **Old Course** is the classic, designed along the lines of a challenging British course. A recent

FARO'S COURSES

Useful telephone numbers:
San Lorenzo –
tel: 289 396 522;
Pinheiros Altos –
tel: 289 394 340;
Quinta do Lago North –
tel: 289 390 700;
Quinta do Lago South –
tel: 289 390 700;
Vale do Lobo –
tel: 289 393 939.

major revamp has put it back in the premier league and, if anything, it demands more accuracy (tel: 289 322 650). Designed by Frank Pennick and Robert Trent Jones, the **Pinhal** course has also undergone substantial remodelling. Less demanding than the Old Course, it still demands plenty of accuracy (tel: 289 321 562). As the name suggests, the **Laguna** incorporates plenty of water hazards in a flat layout characterized by wide fairways (tel: 289 380 724). The latest addition to Vilamoura's portfolio is the **Millennium** course, set in beautifully landscaped surroundings and, along with the Laguna, particularly appealing for holiday golfers rather than experts (tel: 289 310 188).

Pine Cliffs: This is one of the most attractive golf courses in the Algarve, laid out on a gently undulating site behind the red sandstone cliffs overlooking Falésia beach. The nine-hole course contains some challenges – the sixth hole requires a 205m (673ft) carrying shot across a ravine to land on a narrow green by the Sheraton Hotel (tel: 289 501 090).

Balaia Golf Village: Near Albufeira, this nine-hole course is ideal for beginners or for practice rounds (tel: 289 570 442).

Salgados: Located between Albufeira and Armação de Pera, this 6000m (6562yd) course is not long but demands accurate drives to avoid the water hazards. The 15th fairway runs alongside the beach (tel: 289 591 964).

Vale de Milho: All nine holes are par threes but water hazards demand careful play. It's a good place to practise short iron shots and enjoy the landscaped waterfalls and sea views. The course was designed by David Thomas, who was also responsible for the Brabazon in Britain, which has regularly played host to the Ryder Cup (tel: 282 358 502).

Below: *The ravines at Vale do Lobo.*

Pinta: An 18-hole course which has gained a reputation for excellent playing conditions. Designed by Ronald Fream, the course runs through an olive grove where some trees are 700 years old (tel: 282 340 900).

Gramacho: This course has 18 sets of tees and 18 full-sized greens on a nine-hole course. Ronald Fream designed this innovative layout which includes mature olive trees, stone wall hazards, a lake and natural bunkers (tel: 282 340 900).

Western Algarve

Alto Golf: The last course to be designed by the legendary Henry Cotton, this 18-hole parkland course is situated near Alvor, and boasts glorious views of the Monchique hills and the bay of Lagos. With its winding fairways and undulating greens, it offers a test of skill to low handicap players but also a pleasant game to average ability golfers. The 16th hole, known as the Giant, is said to be the longest in Europe – 604m (1982ft) and a par five (tel: 282 416 913).

Penina: Another Henry Cotton masterpiece, the Penina was the first course to be built in the Algarve, and has been completely renovated. The main 18-hole championship course has hosted the Portuguese Open. Set amid mature trees with wide greens and largely flat (the land was originally a rice farm), it incorporates several streams and lakes. The elevated greens play true and encourage attacking play (tel: 282 415 415).

Palmares: This lovely course just east of Lagos, famous for its almond blossom in spring, hosts an annual Almond Blossom tournament. Five of the 18 holes are situated on sand dunes which make up the long sandy beach of Meia Praia. The remaining 13 holes are set among undulating hills and valleys. The variety of the terrain, from the greens to the hillside slopes, as well as the beautiful views of sea and mountains, make the Palmares an ideal course for the holiday golfer. It was designed by Frank

Below: Good riders can enjoy a canter on one of the fine Lusitano horses found in the Algarve.

Penninck (tel: 282 762 961). Just west of Lagos is **Boavista**, a scenic 18-hole course with lovely views designed for the average player (tel: 282 782 151).

Parque da Floresta: The most westerly course in the Algarve is the Parque da Floresta set in the hills behind the fishing village of Salema. The 18 holes run across and through eucalyptus-filled valleys and ravines. Drives must cross a vineyard, a flower garden and

various water hazards. Designed by Spanish architect Pepe Gancedo, the course requires some finesse as well as power, and the latter is certainly required on the opening hole which is 516m (1702ft) long, and offers a challenging shot over a ravine to the safety of the green (tel: 282 695 335).

Above: *The bullfight is a bloody spectacle.*

Eastern Algarve

Benamor Golf: Located between Tavira and the hills, this new course is laid on undulating land with lovely views on all sides (tel: 281 320 880).

Quinta da Ria and Quinta de Cima: Two new 18-hole courses between Tavira and Vila Nova de Cacela (tel: 281 950 580).

Castro Marim Golfe: Set in the quiet hills north of Castro Marim this new 18-hole course promises to play as well as it looks (tel: 281 510 330).

Bullfighting

Bullfighting in Portugal differs in many respects from the better known Spanish spectacle. The bull is fought mainly from horseback where the *cavaleiro* plants *bandarilhas* (barbed darts) into its neck muscles in a display of superb horsemanship and daring. After this the bull is wrestled to the ground by *forcados*, a group of athletic young men. A

LUSITANO – THE ROYAL HORSE

The mount of kings and cavalry officers, the Portuguese Lusitano is a breed with a proud pedigree; the **National Stud** was founded in 1748. This horse is an excellent lightweight riding horse, standing around 15.2 hands and normally grey, brown or bay. It has plenty of quality as its ancestors were the superb **Arab** and **Barb** horses brought to Portugal by the Moors. Fast and intelligent but with a friendly nature, you'll find plenty of Lusitanos in riding schools. This splendid horse also takes part in dressage displays.

COFFEE BREAK

Visiting the coffee shop is part of the Portuguese way of life. If you wish to follow suit, don't just ask for a coffee, ask for a:
Bica • Small strong expresso
Bica cheia • Expresso with extra water
Bica dupla • Double expresso
Bica pingada • With a drop of milk
Café com leite • Coffee with milk
Meia de leite • Half milk, half coffee
Garoto • Expresso with milk
Café gelado • Iced coffee

subsequent bull will be fought Spanish style on foot with the cape, but the death blow is symbolic.

Bullfighting posters claim that the bull is not killed. Half killed is more accurate, and it will be slaughtered shortly after it leaves the ring exhausted and dripping with blood. There is less brutality than in the Spanish version; the bull is not lanced by a *picador* and the crowd does not exult in the moment of death, but it is still a gory business. The main bullrings are in Albufeira, Lagos, Quarteira and Vila Real de Santo António.

Football

Football is a Portuguese obsession, but the most successful clubs in the country are in the north. If you want to see a match there are professional teams at Faro, Lagos, Portimão and Vila Real de Santo António. **Snooker** is the most popular indoor pastime and many bars have tables.

Food and Drink

Below: *No need for fancy cooking when you can eat fish straight from the sea.*

Food is one of the great pleasures of a holiday in the Algarve. This is not a place where you can expect much sophistication or *haute cuisine*, although there are some international-class restaurants in or near the top hotels and five-star developments such as Quinta do Lago and Vale do Lobo.

If you enjoy the taste of fresh **seafood** and locally produced organically grown **vegetables** which are full of flavour, this is just the place for you. Locals however complain that some restaurants now use vegetables imported from Spain. These may be more uniform in size and shape, but are instantly recognizable because they taste so bland. If you're self-catering buy vegetables from the market rather than a supermarket – they are not only cheaper but you are guaranteed local produce.

Fish is often at its best simply grilled over charcoal. A typical, delicious and cheap meal to order is fresh grilled sardines served with salad and crusty country bread.

More elaborate seafood dishes include *arroz de marisco* (seafood rice), *amêijoas na cataplana* (stewed clams, spicy sausage, ham, garlic and onions), and *bacalhau à brás* (cod, potatoes and scrambled egg). Instead of steak, try chicken, pork, lamb, kid and rabbit – they are better choices for carnivores.

Portions are large, and you may want to forgo a starter (bread, fish pâté and olives are included in the cover charge) to leave space for one of the delicious Portuguese **cakes** made from almonds, eggs, sugar and butter. *Pastel de nata* (custard tart), *tarte de amêndoa* (almond cake) and *tarte de laranja* (orange cake) are all worth trying.

Most of the **wine** drunk in the Algarve comes from further north. The red wines from the Alentejo should be sampled, while light white *vinho verde* is a delicious summer wine and goes well with fish. Rosés tend be on the sweet side. Although not well known beyond the borders of their own country, most Portuguese table wines are generally of excellent quality. If you order the house wine in most restaurants, you may not be amazed but you will rarely be disappointed, and the low price will certainly astound you.

After dinner, enjoy a glass of vintage port or sweet madeira, or try the schnapps-like *medronho* or *amêndoa amarga*, a clear spirit distilled from almonds. Local brandy is good (Macieira is a reliable brand), as is the local lager-type beer.

Above: *An alfresco lunch of grilled sardines, salad, potatoes and light white wine.*

FISH

Here's a quick guide to the most popular seafood:
Bacalhau • Dried cod
Linguado • Dover sole
Pargo • Bream
Camarões • Shrimps
Gambas • Prawns
Mexilhões • Mussels
Sardinhas • Sardines
Lulas • Squid
Atum • Tuna
Alibute • Halibut
Salmonete • Red mullet
Robalo • Bass
Amêijoas • Clams
Caranguejo • Crab
Cavala • Mackerel
Espadarte • Swordfish
Espada • Scabbard fish

Azulejos

Nobody can agree on the derivation of the term *azulejo*. It may come from the Portuguese word for blue, *azul*, or from the Arabic *al-Zulaij*, meaning mosaic. These decorative tiles first became popular in the 16th century, with blue, yellow and green the most common colours. By the end of the 17th century, representational art had replaced floral and geometric patterns as the current fashion. Scenes from the Bible and the lives of the saints decorated churches, while great moments of Portuguese history enlivened public buildings. The prevailing colour was now cobalt blue and white. In the 19th century Art Nouveau saw a return to colour, with mythical figures and medieval romanticism being the main themes. The techniques and artistry used to produce *azulejos* are carried through today to other ceramic articles which are widely sold throughout Portugal. Decorative tiles, bowls and plates are perhaps the most tasteful and lovely souvenirs of the Algarve you can take home with you.

Architecture in the Algarve

The 1755 earthquake that devastated Lisbon also destroyed much of the Algarve's architectural heritage. Most of the fine old buildings which remain in the Algarve are churches. These display a fascinating patchwork of styles which reflects centuries of renovations, additions and remodelling. **Romanesque** is the term applied to the solidly built, fortress-like 12th-century churches constructed after the reconquest of Portugal. The **Gothic** style, with its characteristic buttresses and pointed arches, was in vogue during the 13th and 14th centuries.

During the 15th and 16th centuries Portugal developed its own unique architectural style, called **Manueline**, after Manuel the Fortunate who reigned from 1495–1521. The excitement of those heady times, when Portugal ruled the seas and was the richest nation on earth, is reflected in the exuberant architecture. The shape remained basically Gothic, but the style became much less formal and incorporated many exotic oriental touches. Columns and doorways were modelled into twisting ropes, and the nautical theme was continued in knots, fishes, chains and anchors. Floral motifs too were often worked into extravagant designs.

From the mid-16th century onwards the Classical symmetry of the **Renaissance** period took over, to be followed a century later by the excessively ornate Baroque interiors of the churches of that period, with their gilded

Opposite: *Graceful filigree chimneys are one of the highlights of the Algarve's vernacular architecture.*
Right: *The design of these door knockers in a Ferragudo sidestreet dates from Moorish times.*

woodwork and ostentatious statues. The *igreja toda de ouro*, where the interior is completely covered in gilded woodwork, is unique to Portugal. The period of rebuilding following the Great Earthquake is dominated by neoclassical architecture (known in Portugal as **Pomabaline**, after the Marquês de Pombal) characterized by simplicity of form.

It is, however, the small details of vernacular architecture, most of which are derived from the **Moors**, which are often the most interesting in the Algarve. The influence of the Moors can be seen today in the wonderful tiles, or *azulejos* as they are known in Portugal

(*see* page 32), which decorate everything from street signs and park benches to opulent church interiors. Throughout the Algarve you will see charming decorative chimneys in an astonishing range of shapes and ornate patterns. The door knockers shaped like tiny hands, which you can see on old doorways, are Moorish too, and represent the hand of Fatima which wards off the evil eye.

Gaily painted or whitewashed cubist houses are more reminiscent of a kasbah than anything European. Roofs are flat and act as a handy terrace for drying fruits. They are protected by small latticed walls, often ornately carved and known as *platibandas*, which allow the air to circulate around the roof but prevent the fruit from being blown away in a strong gust of wind. Even modern luxury villas have an exotic Moorish look, with their distinctive filigree chimneys, arched windows, red tiled roofs, shady courtyards and latticework balconies.

MUSEUMS

Many (but not all) museums close on Mondays; some also close on local saints' days and public holidays. If you are driving a long way to visit a specific museum, a call in advance to the local tourist office could save a wasted journey. Charges are generally very reasonable. In many of the museums labelling and information are only available in Portuguese. Notable exceptions to this include the **Archaeology Museum** in Silves, the **Museum of Discoveries** in Lagos, Évora's **Municipal Museum** and the **Convento da Nossa Senhora da Conceição** in Beja.

2
In and
Around Faro

The capital of the Algarve and its political and administrative centre, Faro has a population of about 50,000. With an international airport, it's the first point of contact with the Algarve for many visitors. However, in their rush to the seaside few stop and look around.

Despite Faro's long history – Romans are said to have founded a town here called Ossonoba and it was also a Moorish town – much of what remains dates from the 1800s and 1900s. Faro was devastated by the 1755 earthquake. Nevertheless, the **Old Town** is worth a visit.

Immediately west of Faro is the **Golden Coast**, where you find the top two private developments in the Algarve: **Quinta do Lago** and **Vale do Lobo**, with their millionaires' villas and manicured golf courses. Half an hour after landing at the airport, second home owners from Britain and northern European countries can be sipping a gin and tonic on the patio without the bother of lengthy transfers.

The region has four of the Algarve's top **golf courses**: San Lorenzo, Pinheiros Altos, Quinta do Lago and Vale do Lobo. Tennis players and horse riders also have a wealth of opportunities in the area to enjoy their sport.

The coastline changes here from the low-lying sand bars and lagoons of the eastern Algarve to the rockier west. But beautiful beaches are common to both regions.

Situated inland, **Loulé** is one of the most authentic and interesting towns in the Algarve, and the foothills of the **Serra do Caldeirão** offer wonderful scenery and plenty of pretty villages.

CLIMATE

Average temperatures don't give the whole story. In July and August in the Algarve you can expect afternoon temperatures to reach 28°C (83°F), with **warm** nights where the temperature does not fall below 20°C (68°F). January is the **coolest** month, with temperatures reaching an average high of 15°C (60°F) during the day, and falling by night to 9°C (48°F). **Frost** is not unknown but is very rare at sea level.

Opposite: *Estói Palace dates from the 18th century; the grounds are full of tiles and neoclassical statues.*

Right: *Boats take visitors to the nearby offshore islands from Faro.*

FARO

If arriving by car, follow the signs to the port and railway station and park near the waterfront. The café in the gardens facing the harbour is a good spot to have a coffee and get your bearings.

Maritime Museum ★★

The Maritime Museum is next to the harbourmaster's office. It has scale models of caravels and galleons, plus fishing tackle, tuna harpoons and fish traps, nets and cages. Open 14:30–16:30 Monday–Friday.

Cross the square and walk through the Arco da Vila, passing the Tourist Office just to your left. The imposing Italianate archway was commissioned by the Bishop of Faro to replace the original medieval archway after the Great Earthquake of 1755. The statue above the arch is of St Thomas Aquinas; storks nest in the belfry on top.

Cathedral ★★

Faro's cathedral is in the Largo da Sé, which also contains the former Bishop's Palace and town hall. The statues in the square are of Bishop Francisco Gomes, who masterminded the reconstruction of Faro after the earthquake, and Dom Afonso III, who completed the reconquest of Portugal by finally driving the Moors out of the Algarve.

The cathedral was built in 1251 on the site of a mosque, but was badly damaged in the earthquake.

DON'T MISS

★★ Faro: take a walk around the old town.
★★ Estói: the crumbling palace.
★★ Loulé: good shopping and sightseeing.
★★ Serra do Caldeirão: exploring this lovely region.
★★ Quinta do Lago and **Vale do Lobo:** see how the other half live.
★★ Almancil: *azulejo*-covered interior of São Lourenço.

The outside is heavily remodelled Romanesque and Gothic, while the interior, with its gilded woodwork, has Renaissance and Baroque elements. There are panoramic views over the town and the lagoons and salt marshes of the Ria Formosa Nature Reserve. Open 10:00–17:00 Monday–Saturday.

Archaeology Museum ★★

The 16th-century Convent of Nossa Senhora da Assunção behind the cathedral houses the Archaeology Museum. The most striking exhibits are Roman mosaics and a collection of *azulejos* (see page 32) dating from the 15th century onwards. The graceful arches of the cloisters are worth seeing in their own right. Open 10:00–18:00 Tuesday–Sunday.

HISTORY

It was the **Moors** who gave Faro its name and developed it as a city. Faro was also their last important stronghold in the Algarve, only capitulating in 1249 – a century after Christian forces had taken Lisbon. In 1596, during Spain's 60-year rule of Portugal, Faro was sacked and set ablaze by English forces under Queen Elizabeth's favourite, the Earl of Essex. The city was rebuilt only to be destroyed yet again in the Great Earthquake of 1755.

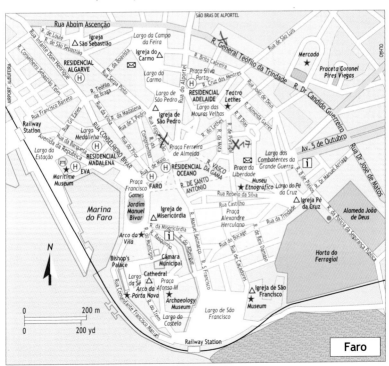

VANISHED PREDATOR

As recently as the 1950s wolves could be found throughout Portugal. Twenty years ago their distinctive howl could still be heard in the Alentejo. Now less than 200 remain, mainly in the mountains of the north east. In the Algarve they are remembered only in names such as **Vale do Lobo** – Valley of the Wolf. In 1989 a **Wolf Recovery Centre** was set up near Lisbon to care for orphaned pups and wolves rescued from illegal traps. You can support the work of the centre by making donations to the world-wide **Born Free Foundation**.

Largo de São Francisco Church ★

Leaving the old town by the Arco da Repousa, cross the empty Largo de São Francisco and visit the church of the same name next to a monastery, which is currently being restored to house Faro's Hotel and Catering School. Inside are fine gilded and lacquered woodcarvings, and blue *azulejo* tiles depicting scenes from the life of St Francis.

The main **shopping** streets are Ruas Vasco da Gama and Santo António. At nearby Praça Ferreira de Almeida you'll find a variety of inexpensive, authentic restaurants.

ALONG THE COAST
Quinta do Lago ★★

Perhaps the most exclusive resort development in the Algarve, this 645ha (2000 acres) estate has maintained a low density building policy. Villas and apartments are tucked away behind stands of umbrella pines creating a pleasant and exclusive ambience. Fine **shops**, first-class **restaurants**, a **beach** along with **golf**, tennis, riding, squash and water sports are all on site.

Almost half of the development is devoted to golf fairways and greens and it contains some of the Algarve's top courses, including **Quinta do Lago**, **San Lorenzo** and **Pinheiros Altos**.

It's more than just a golfers' paradise, however. Migrating birds find a safe haven in the westernmost corner of the **Ria Formosa Nature Reserve**. Quinta do Lago's management has created a nature trail through the estuaries, dunes and marshes which lie inland from the beach, and has also planted nest boxes to encourage smaller birds to settle in the area.

Vale do Lobo ★★

The name 'Vale do Lobo' means Valley of the Wolf, but the inhabitants of this 400ha (100-acre) luxury develop-ment could be described as fat cats. Having said that, the luxury villas and apartments do look attractive. The Moorish influence is clearly evident in the arches, lat-ticed balconies and red tiled roofs, and the grounds have been well landscaped with shrubs and flowers.

BIRDS

Birds to look out for on the nature trail (and anywhere in the Ria Formosa Nature Reserve) include the hoopoe, with its zebra-striped wings and ostentatious crest, the unmistakable stork and long-legged black-winged stilts. Plovers, sandpipers, little herons and great tits are just some of the other birds you might see. Ducks include coots, mallards and teal.

Many of the owners are not year-round residents, but rent their private properties through Vale do Lobo's administration or holiday companies, so the area always plays host to a general mix of regular guests and transient visitors. All the necessities and services are laid on for guests – from private emergency services, banks and shops to restaurants, bars and a luxury hotel, the Dona Filipa. It is a fully functioning resort in its own right. There is also a 5km (3-mile) beach with a water-sports centre.

The superb **sports facilities** on the doorstep are the prime attraction for most guests. There are two 18-hole courses which include the world-famous 16th hole on the **Royal Course**, needing a strong drive across two ravines on the cliffs. The new **Ocean Course**, the last to be designed by the great Henry Cotton, provides attractive links-style golf, less demanding than the Royal Course.

Barringtons is a health club with indoor and outdoor pools, gym, exercise classes, squash courts and golf driving range. The Tennis Academy offers tennis holidays for all levels, from beginners to club competitors. There are a dozen courts where coaching courses, tournaments and specialized clinics are run. Non-residents can use the facilities on offer – but at a price.

Around Faro

FEEL THE FORCE

Locals and visitors claim there is a mysterious force at work on the N270 road from Boliqueime to Loulé. On a hill just past the Eurocampina factory, a car put into neutral will, witnesses claim, not only stop without the use of brakes but reverse back up the hill! One theory is that the nearby quarry has uncovered some kind of magnetic force; the more sedate alternative suggests it's all an optical illusion. If you do try this out yourself, keep an eye on the traffic.

Below: *Haggling over prices in the Gypsy Market is all part of the fun – but remember the stallholders have had plenty of practice.*

Almancil ★

This village west of Faro straddles the EN125 and consists mainly of bars and restaurants serving the surrounding private developments. But just to the east (situated on the northern side of the main road) you will find **São Lourenço**, one of the Algarve's most interesting churches. The church has a gilded altar and is covered with blue and white 18th-century *azulejos*, depicting the life of St Laurence.

Loulé ★★

Loulé is located 18km (11 miles) northeast of Faro. Most visitors arrive on Saturday to see the weekly **Gypsy Market**, but in fact Loulé is a rewarding town to visit any day of the week. In any case, the Gypsy Market is overrated unless you want to buy lace tablecloths, bags, belts, shoes and T-shirts at prices higher than in the shops.

The stallholders are interesting, however. Unmistakably different to the Portuguese, with their striking profiles and dark complexions, the women wear long skirts and the men dusty cowboy boots, although these days goods are moved around by transit van.

Of equal interest is the morning municipal **market** just off the Praça da República, where you can buy the very freshest organic fruit, vegetables, bunches of herbs and dried fruit and nut mix. Tender-hearted visitors should avert their eyes (and ears) from the shoeboxes full of squeaking chicks and ducklings or lop-eared baby rabbits.

Loulé is a town where traditions of **craftsmanship** live on. You can see artisans working brass, copper, tin and wrought iron in the streets around the market. Pottery, wax candles, shoes, cane furniture and harnesses are also made here.

The tourist office is located within the walls of the **castle**, which is of Moorish origin. Little remains but the view from the ramparts. The highlight of the small museum (located next to the tourist office) is the reconstruction of a traditional Algarve kitchen.

The parish church of **São Clemente** encapsulates a mixture of styles, ranging from 13th-century Gothic through to later Manueline embellishments. The latter are particularly noticeable in the side chapel of São Brás. The tall bell tower with its onion dome is all that remains of the **Mosque of Loulé**. Formerly a minaret, it was Christianized by placing the Portuguese coat of arms on the vault of the steeple. The bells and clock were added in the 1500s.

Opposite is a lovely little shaded garden which goes by the intriguing name of **Jardim dos Amuados** – Garden of the Sulky Ones.

The **Church of São Francisco** in Rua Vasco da Gama has a pelican-shaped tabernacle, while the walls in the Church of Nossa Senhora da Conceição near the castle, are almost entirely covered with blue and white *azulejos* depicting Bible scenes.

Despite (or perhaps because of) being a hard-working town, Loulé lets its hair down every year during **Carnival** – five days of mayhem which come before Lent. The 40 days of fasting which were once traditional in the run up to Easter (carnival comes from *carne vale* – farewell to meat) are not followed with any great rigour in the Algarve, but the party lingers on. You can expect to see floats, fireworks, flower battles, fancy dress, drinking and dancing in the streets, and also water and flour bombs aimed at friends but often missing their targets!

THE SOVEREIGN MOTHER

Altogether more solemn occasions than Carnival are the annual **Mãe Soberana** processions. On Easter Sunday, a 16th-century statue of Mãe Soberana (the Sovereign Mother) with her dead son is carried from her shrine on a hillside into town. Two weeks later she is returned. Although Christian, this ceremony is based on pagan rituals which celebrated the spring and the bounty of the Great Goddess.

Below: *Loulé's parish church is an eclectic mix of architectural styles.*

Above: *This charming nymph is one of the many neoclassical statues decorating the grounds of the palace of Estói.*

ESTÓI AND AROUND ★★

The most interesting Roman remains in the Algarve are at **Milreu**. Archaeologists excavating the site over the last hundred years have found that it was occupied by a succession of buildings dating from the 1st century AD. The main ruins are of a large country villa with columns surrounding a central courtyard.

On the west side was a bathhouse with hot and cold bathrooms and benches for massage and relaxation. The hot bathroom had underfloor heating as a byproduct of the furnace used to boil cauldrons of water. Some fish mosaics remain, although most of the finds (statues and ceramics) are now in Faro and Lagos museums. This was a sophisticated villa for the times and no doubt belonged to an aristocrat. The standard of living was superior to anything found in the Algarve in the Middle Ages, and probably higher than that experienced by isolated farming communities even today.

To the right of the villa is the surviving wall of a temple to a local water cult or deity whose name has not survived. This was turned into a church by the Romans' successors, the Visigoths.

In Estói, park by the church and head for the wrought iron gates at the end of the street. This is the **Palace of Estói**, built by the **Counts of Carvalhal** in the 18th century. It has now been turned into a *pousada* (historic hotel) and, at the time of writing, it is unclear whether the gardens will still be open to the public. If not, consider stopping for lunch (or perhaps just coffee) to gain access.

The neoclassical façade is a pink and white confection and the gardens are wonderfully evocative. The counts obviously lived in some style here, as the Romans had done earlier in nearby Milreu. The *azulejos*, nymphs, statues, fountains and paths through orange trees are quite delightful. Steps lead down to a grotto with statues of Diana, Venus and the Three Graces.

From Estói you can drive up the N2 road into some of the loveliest countryside in the Algarve. North of São Brás de Alportel the road climbs up into the **Serra do Caldeirão** and the vegetation becomes lusher and more abundant.

The air is fragrant with the smell of pines and eucalyptus, and alive with the sound of birdsong. In spring there are wild flower meadows where the trees open out – red splashes of poppies and swathes of yellow broom.

There's a glorious view from the Miradouro de Caldeirão just north of Vale da Rosa – not a village, but a vantage point overlooking rolling hills. It's a challenging drive around hairpin bends, and the road is poorly surfaced with the original cobbles showing through in places. But it's worth the drive.

Salir ★

All that remains of the once-mighty Moorish castle here are fragments of the walls, which provide panoramic views over the countryside. You can see tiny smallholdings, each one providing enough to feed a single family. These often consist of a few rows of vegetables, a lemon and orange tree and some straggly vines. Salir itself is a spotless little village where the whitewashed houses contrast with vivid splashes of geraniums.

To the south, **Querença** is a hilltop village with an *azulejo*-backed village spring and a neat church. Should you feel the need to stretch your legs and visit a quiet beauty spot, take the road to **Aldeia da Tôr** through the typical landscape of the Barrocal, with limestone outcrops and remains of hillside terraces laid down by the Moors.

Turn left towards Querença, and after about 3km (2 miles) look out for the signpost pointing left to the **Fonte de Benemola**. Follow the track along the river. When the path divides bear left, and you will come to a picnic area. Further on you will find the *fonte* (spring) and stepping stones to ford the stream, so that you may return along the other bank. The walk is no more than 4km (2½ miles) but takes you deep into lovely countryside.

> **PICNIC FOOD**
>
> You can get all your picnic ingredients at the supermarket; otherwise shop locally at the bakery, greengrocer's and *charcuteria* – the latter a delicatessen as well as a butchery. Here you can buy cold roast chicken (*frango*), garlic sausage (*chouriço*), and cartons of prepared salad and cheese (*queijo*). If you don't know the name for something tasty looking, just point and say 'Queria aquilo.' 'I would like that.' With some fruit for dessert and a bottle of wine, you're all set!

Below: *Estói Palace, where the Counts of Carvalhal enjoyed a decadent lifestyle, is now an empty shell but there are plans to restore the interior.*

In and Around Faro at a Glance

BEST TIMES TO VISIT

Every season in the Algarve has its good points. **Spring** is memorable for its almond blossom, followed shortly afterwards by wild flowers of every hue. It can be hot in **summer** but there is normally a refreshing breeze on the coast. This is when the water is at its warmest and the beaches are packed with families. As with spring, **autumn** sees ideal temperatures for walking, golf and other outdoor activities, but November and December can be wet. Mild winter days when you can sit at outdoor cafés in shirt sleeves are a real tonic if arriving from colder climes, but you can't count on warm dry weather – so treat it as a bonus.

GETTING THERE

Most visitors to the Algarve arrive at the **Faro international airport**, 6km (4 miles) from the town centre, where, during the summer months, flights land 24 hours a day. You will find tourist information, medical facilities, duty-free shopping, banking and a range of food outlets, plus specially designated areas for children. Shuttle Direct (www.shuttledirect. com) runs pre-booked shuttle buses to the main resorts. Package tours generally include transport to and from your accommodation. There are **taxis** and some **buses** to Faro town centre. Silves and Albufeira are both served by the local **railway**

line, with connections from Faro in the east and Lagos in the west. The stations are, however, a few kilometres away from the town. The Faro–Lagos express bus service calls at Montechoro, Albufeira, Ferreiras, Armação de Pêra and Lagoa.

GETTING AROUND

Buses connect most of the major resorts in the Algarve and also inland towns such as Silves and Monchique. Local buses also provide 'hopper' services between the main resorts and also from the coast inland to Silves. The local tourist office normally has up-to-date details. Roadside bus stops are marked by the word *paragem* on a sign. Check local timetables before travelling – these are normally available at tourist information offices as well as bus and train stations. The **local train service**, which links Lagos in the west with Vila Real de Santo António in the east, is interesting if a little slow. In some towns – most notably Silves and Albufeira – the station is several kilometres from the town centre. **Taxis** are plentiful and can be found in ranks or ordered by telephone.

WHERE TO STAY

LUXURY
Pousada de São Bras, tel: 289 842 305. The first *pousada* to be built in the Algarve, this is in a quiet country town of the same name close to Estói and Milreu. Comfortable

accommodation, pool and lots of specialities in the restaurant.
Hotel Quinta do Lago, tel: 289 350 350, www.hotelquintadolago.com Possibly the top hotel in the Algarve region; and is a member of the Leading Hotels of the World.
Le Meridien Dona Filipa, Vale do Lobo, tel: 289 357 200, www.starwoodhotels.com A fine five-star hotel with privileged access to the area's best golf courses.

MID-RANGE
Estalagem Aeromar, Praia de Faro, tel: 289 817 189, www.aeromar.net A comfortable and rather unpretentious hotel with rooms with views over the sea or lagoon.
Hotel Faro, Praça Dom Francisco Gomes 2, tel: 289 830 830. A four-star hotel in an excellent location and a good meeting place.
Hotel Eva, Avenida de la Republica, Faro, tel: 289 001 000. Big rooms, views of harbour, near bus station.
Monte do Casal, Estói, tel: 289 991 503. Former farmhouse, now posh B&B. Good food, English owner.
Quinta da Calma, Almansil, tel: 289 393 741, www. quinta-da-calma.com Yoga and other alternative therapies are offered here, as well as vegetarian food, and accommodation in little cabins.

Loulé Jardim, Praça Manuel de Arriago, Loulé, tel: 289 413 094. A modern three-star hotel with rooftop pool and friendly staff.

BUDGET
Residencial Algarve, Rua Infante Dom Henrique 52, Faro, tel: 289 895 700.
Pensão Madalena Residencial, Rua Conselheiro Bivar 109, Faro, tel: 289 805 806.

WHERE TO EAT

Almancil
Here can be found top-class restaurants serving the well-heeled clients of Quinta do Lago and Vale do Lobo and, of course, with prices to match. You can expect inter-national cuisine rather than Portuguese.

Lisboa Antigua, Avenida 5 Outobro 85, tel: 289 391 883. Traditional dishes are served here, and there is *fado* music twice a week.
Julia's, Praia Garrao, tel: 289 396 512. Has a beachfront location and is a favourite with golfers.

Faro
Adega Dois Irmãos, Largo de Terreiro do Bispo, tel: 289 823 337. An established favourite, specializing in seafood.
Restaurante A Taska, Rua do Alportel 38, tel: 289 824 739. This restaurant is a local favourite.

Praia do Faro
Camané, tel: 289 817 539. Enjoy fresh fish by the sea, in a restaurant much frequented by celebrities.

Querença (near Loulé)
Moinho ti Casinha, tel: 289 438 108. Traditional meat dishes in the countryside.

Loulé
Restaurante O Pescador, Rua José Geurreiro, tel: 289 462 821. By the market, this place serves good seafood at reasonable prices.
Restaurante Bica Velha, Rua Martim Moniz 17, tel: 289 463 376. Not cheap, but best for Algarve specialities.

TOURS AND EXCURSIONS

Megatur, Rua Conselheiro de Bivar 80, Faro, tel: 289 807 485, has a good choice of organized excursions to all corners of the Algarve.
Almargem, tel: 289 412 959; phone for details of the Saturday walks organized by this environmental group.

SPORTS

Pinetrees Riding Centre, Estrada do Anção, Almancil,

tel: 289 394 489, www.pinetreesridingcentre.com This is a well-established school with an English owner. It has been approved by the Association of British Riding Schools.
Almancil Karting, Sitio das Pereiras, Almancil, tel: 289 399 899, www.mundokarting.pt Karts for kids and adults, two tracks, boating lake and Wild West theme park.

Beaches
Faro has its own beach, 7km (4½ miles) out of town, just past the airport, on a long narrow spit connected to the mainland by a causeway. It's a jolly place, with good swimming and plenty of bars and restaurants, and is packed with locals at week-ends. Ferries run from the harbour in town to other beaches at regular intervals from June to September.

USEFUL CONTACTS

Tourist Offices
Faro: Rua da Misericórdia 8–12, tel: 289 803 604.
Loulé: Avenida 25 de Abril, tel: 289 463 900.

FARO	J	F	M	A	M	J	J	A	S	O	N	D
AVERAGE TEMP. °C	12	13	14	16	18	22	24	24	23	19	16	13
AVERAGE TEMP. °F	54	55	58	61	65	72	75	75	73	66	61	55
SEA TEMP. °C	12	16	17	17	19	20	21	23	22	21	16	15
SEA TEMP. °F	54	61	63	63	66	68	70	73	72	70	61	60
RAINFALL mm	70	52	72	31	21	5	1	1	17	51	65	67
RAINFALL in	2.8	2.1	2.8	1.2	0.8	0.2	-	-	0.7	2.0	2.6	2.6
DAYS OF RAINFALL	9	7	10	6	4	1	-	-	2	6	8	9

3
Central Algarve

The Central Algarve is the province's holiday heartland, and the entire coastal strip is geared towards tourism. In addition to dozens of sandy beaches sheltered by honey-coloured cliffs, you'll find a wide choice of water sports and amusements to keep you busy.

Purists scoff at the region and claim it has been over-commercialized, but it remains popular. It has the country's largest concentration of hotels and apartments. Thousands of holiday-makers stay here every year: in bustling **resorts** such as Albufeira, Quarteira and Armação de Pêra, quieter spots such as Carvoeiro and Ferragudo, or modern developments in São Rafael and Galé.

The Central Algarve is a good choice for families with children, with five **Water Parks** to choose from, while golfers have their pick of a dozen courses. This area has more year-round life than more authentic but less popular resorts to the east and west. This is also a good base from which to explore other parts of the Algarve, as the entire coast from Sagres to Vila Real de Santo António lies within day-trip range. Inland you can see the once-great castles of Silves and Paderne, as well as sleepy little towns such as Lagoa and Alcantarilha.

In addition to Portuguese cuisine you can dine out on fish and chips, burgers, bacon and eggs, curry, pasta and pizzas, and order a pint of beer in an English-style pub. Music bars and discos provide a lively nightlife scene. This is not a place to go to get away from it all but it has plenty of devoted fans.

DON'T MISS

★★★ **Silves:** visit the atmospheric castle.
★★ **Guia:** the chicken *piri piri* is outstanding.
★★ **Beaches:** explore the lovely beaches between Armação de Pêra and Carvoeiro.
★★ **Paderne:** take a walk in the nearby countryside.
★★ **Alte:** enjoy a picnic by the river.

Opposite: *A stroll through Albufeira's old town gives you a feeling of what life was like before tourism took over.*

ORIGINS OF ALBUFEIRA

Albufeira's origins are unknown, but it was an important port in Roman times and was called Baltum. In the 8th century the Moors renamed it *al-Buhera* – literally, 'castle on the sea'. Over the next four centuries the town thrived thanks to trade links with North Africa. It was one of the very last Moorish strongholds in the Algarve, only finally falling to the Portuguese in 1250. With its trade links severed, the town fell into decay; it was flattened by the 1755 earthquake and then virtually destroyed by Miguelite supporters during the War of the Two Brothers.

Below: *Local artists display their wares on the terrace just above Fishermen's Beach.*

ALBUFEIRA ★★

The largest resort in the Algarve, Albufeira does not have as many permanent residents as Faro, the provincial capital, but the population quadruples to 100,000 and more during the summer influx of tourists. Once an obscure fishing village, it was raised to the status of a city in 1987.

Albufeira is a fully fledged resort with a lively atmosphere. It is also a great favourite with holidaying Portuguese families, and remains open for business in the winter months. The local authorities have gone to a great deal of trouble to improve the resort's looks in recent years; tourism is taken seriously here and it shows. However, despite being the most successful resort in the Algarve, Albufeira has by no means lost all its original charm, and the best place to begin to discover its past is to start off at **Praia dos Barcos**, or Fishermen's Beach.

Show up early and you'll see fishermen unloading their catch; during the day they mend their nets among hordes of sunbathers. On the terrace above the beach are lively restaurants, and on the far right as you face the sea is all that is left of Albufeira's once formidable castle, which was destroyed in the 1755 earthquake. Only a portion remains, and it has now been incorporated into **A Ruina**, a popular restaurant and bar on several levels.

Walk up the Rua Nova beside A Ruina, turn left, and you're in the heart of the **Old Town**, with its steeped cobbled lanes and old houses. The **Misericórdia Chapel** in Rua Henrique Calado dates from the 1500s and is said to have been built on the site of a mosque, but it is closed for restoration.

Continue past the tunnel which leads to the main beach (the tourist office is up on the right) and into Praça Miguel Bombarda; pause for a look at the 16th-century **Church of São Sebastião**, with its Manueline portal and Renaissance side door, gilded altar and statue of Nossa Senhora da Orada with the baby Jesus.

The main **shopping** street is Rua 5 de Outubro, and if you need to update your holiday wardrobe or want to buy stylish ceramics, this is the place to find an assortment of treasures. If you want to pick up some holiday reading material, visit the Algarve Book Centre in Rua da Igreja Nova. **Largo Engenheiro Duarte Pacheco**, the main square to the east, boasts an assortment of souvenir shops, bars and restaurants. This area is the heart of the evening scene, with its lights, music and crowds of party people.

Just to the east of Albufeira are the satellite developments of **Montechoro** and **Praia da Oura**. These developments are connected by the **Strip** – a road running down to the sea which is lined with popular souvenir shops, restaurants and bars. Behind the Strip are acres of holiday flats – there are even some built into the bullring. There's no old town charm here but the beach is excellent.

FAVOURITE DISH

Bacalhau à brás is not only popular with visitors, but is also a favourite supper dish with Portuguese families. To serve four you'll need: 400g (15oz) dried salt cod soaked in water overnight, 500g (18oz) potatoes, 6 eggs, 3 onions, 4 garlic cloves, olive oil, black pepper, parsley and black olives to garnish. Shred the potatoes; fry until golden. Fry onions and garlic; add the flaked cod and potatoes. Place in a casserole, pour over the beaten eggs, and cook in a moderate oven for half an hour. Delicious!

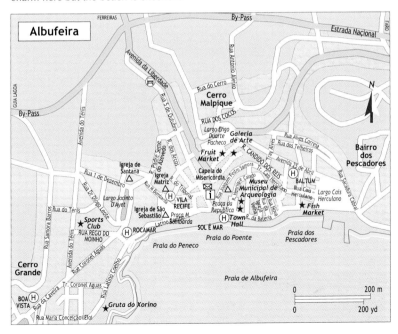

WATER SPORTS

The main water-sport centres
where you can rent equip-
ment are: Albufeira,
Carvoeiro, Lagos, Vilamoura,
Olhão, Armação de Pêra,
Alvor, Praia da Rocha,
Quinta do Lago, Vale do
Lobo, Sagres and Ferragudo.
The most sheltered waters
(good for water-skiing and
novice windsurfers) can be
found in the lagoons of the
eastern Algarve and at
Ferragudo. Surfers catch the
biggest waves on the west
coast, while the rocky western half of the province
provides fascinating territory
for snorkellers.

Below: *The huge
marina is the focal
point of Vilamoura.*

EAST FROM ALBUFEIRA

Between Albufeira and Vilamoura are two of the
Algarve's longest and loveliest beaches: Falésia and
Balaia, which both offer good opportunities for water
sports. Both are backed by relatively sedate modern
developments such as Balaia Village and Olhos de
Agua. The luxury Sheraton Hotel, built in local style
with cool courtyards, fountains and *azulejos*, presides
over the exclusive Pine Cliffs Golf and Country Club.

Vilamoura

Billed as the largest privately developed resort in
Europe, Vilamoura covers 1600ha (4000 acres) of
scrubby land. The centre of the resort is the **marina**,
where multicoloured apartment blocks, hotels and
restaurants cluster around the water's edge. If there is a
unified style (and that's debatable) it could best be
described as undistinguished post-modern architecture.

Inland are rather isolated 'villages' consisting of
apartments and villas. If you stay here a car is a necessity.
This is all part of an ambitious plan to turn Vilamoura
into a 'green town' resort with a permanent population
of 30,000 and an enviable lifestyle.

There are already upwards of 200
shops, restaurants and bars, while the
impressive sports facilities include four
golf courses and the largest marina in
Europe with berths for 1000 boats. Big
game fishing, sailing, windsurfing, water
skiing and diving are all available; land
sports include bowling, jogging along
marked trails, tennis, soccer and riding.

The name Vilamoura means Moorish
Village, but the area was inhabited long
before their time. Excavations just north of
the marina have revealed the ruins of a
Roman villa, baths and farm buildings.
Recovered mosaics, Roman lamps and
Visigothic coins can be seen in a small
museum nearby (open daily 10:00–17:00).

Quarteira

Vilamoura's eastern suburbs merge seamlessly with Quarteira. Forty years ago it was a pretty fishing village but now it's a jumble of tower block apartments and hotels. It is currently deeply unfashionable, so you can pick up some excellent deals on accommodation here. Many of the older apartment blocks now house workers who service the neighbouring more up-market developments; others are rented out to Portuguese holidaymakers. So despite its less than perfect looks, Quarteira is developing a more Portuguese atmosphere. The long sandy beach runs virtually uninterrupted to Faro.

There are two **Water Parks** within easy reach of Quarteira. **Aquashow** is on the road to the EN125, and features a covered wave pool along with extensive play areas for children. Next door is a mini racing track with scaled down Formula One cars, providing lots of thrills for aspiring young racing drivers. **Atlantic Park** is on the EN125 and offers plenty of chutes and slides. In the summer months high divers from Acapulco sometimes put on displays.

DRUG LAWS

Despite the Algarve's cosmopolitan veneer, Portugal is still a conservative society, and visitors suspected of importing recreational drugs (particularly if there is any hint of dealing) will find themselves in trouble. Drug use among the Portuguese is not as widespread as in Spain, but **cannabis** comes in by boat from Morocco to marinas such as Vilamoura. **Cocaine** from South America circulates mainly in Lisbon, and **Ecstasy** is associated with the club scene as it is throughout Europe.

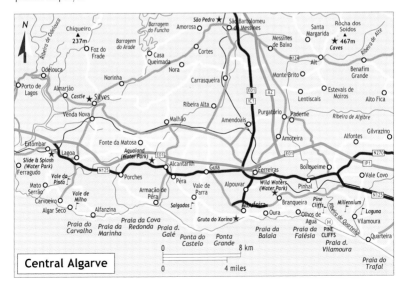

Central Algarve

Above: *São Rafael is one of the most beautiful beaches in the central Algarve.* **Opposite:** *Don't get too close to the cave entrances at Algar Seco if you're snorkelling and the sea is rough!*

CATAPLANA

The *cataplana*, an Algarvian speciality, is a delicious seafood casserole named after the tin or copper pressure-cooker type vessel it's cooked in. There are several varieties but *amêijoas* (clams) are common to all, with other ingredients ranging from spicy sausage to lobster. A *cataplana* for two can usually feed three or four – don't go home without trying one!

WEST FROM ALBUFEIRA

To Albufeira's immediate west are some superb **beaches**, a fact which has not escaped the developers' attention. Almost the whole coastal area to Armação de Pêra has been divided into plots, and villas and apartments are mushrooming. But it's all fairly low density development aimed at those families looking for a quiet holiday.

The first beach you come to is **São Rafael**, a delightful stretch of smooth yellow sand backed by sandstone cliffs. Some sections of cliff have become detached after millennia of weathering, and now stand alone or in arches, providing shade when on the beach, and interesting places to snorkel around when half submerged in water. There's a friendly beach restaurant, and more are springing up behind the beach as the resort develops.

Praia do Castelo is another lovely beach, set in a weathered landscape of sculpted cliffs, grottoes and blowholes. Gently shelving and with lots of shade, it appeals to families with young children.

Further along is **Galé**, backed by small rocks and dunes rather than cliffs. This modern resort has become popular with British families over the last few years. For the time being however the accommodation outstrips the amenities.

Armação de Pêra

LikeAlbufeira, Armação de Pêra is one of the oldest established resorts in the Algarve but, unlike Albufeira Armação is looking her age, a tired and somewhat dowdy old lady.

The beach is enormous and extends all the way down the coast to Galé. Behind it is a rather pleasant promenade, but just inland are cheaply constructed apartment towers. The eastern part of town retains a great deal more character, with fishing boats and plenty of authentic fish restaurants.

The 18th-century fort here, built as a defence against marauding pirates, is described by most guidebooks as 'ruined'. All that remains today is a tiny chapel and some vestiges of the walls.

To the west are cliffs, striking rock formations and tiny sandy coves accessible only by boat. The twin beaches of **Praia Senhora da Rocha** are linked by a tunnel; the name comes from the simple fishermen's chapel perched on the cliffs above. Continuing west are more pretty beaches, but **Albandeira**, **Marinha**, **Benagil**, **Carvalho** and **Centianes** are the best for swimming.

Algar Seco is a wonderfully dramatic outcrop of golden, ochre and russet cliffs, which are holed like a honeycomb but with flat shelves across which you can wander. There are caves, passages through the rock and a 'window' looking out to sea. It's equally dramatic viewed from the sea, and visitors on boat trips from both Armação and Carvoeiro pause here to admire the impressive view. This is also an excellent place to snorkel, and you can enter the sea easily enough just to the west.

THE PIRATES

Armação flourished after its fortress was built in the 18th century to defend it against pirates. These sea wolves began terrorizing southern Spain and Portugal in the 16th century. Based in Tripoli, Algiers and Morocco, the notorious Barbary corsairs looted ships and towns. Captives taken were sold into slavery. The coastline of the Algarve, with its hidden bays, was wide open to attack. It was not until the 19th century that the problem was brought under control, largely thanks to the superior fire power of the French and British navies.

Above: *The beach at Carvoeiro is one of the most photographed scenes in the Algarve.*

Carvoeiro ★

Once a simple fishing village, the hills around Carvoeiro are splashed white with modern villas, but the village itself, tucked in between high cliffs, retains plenty of charm. Local artists sell water colours which encapsulate the village's pretty-as-a-picture appeal.

While it is busy during the height of summer, Carvoeiro is a stylish resort with several golf courses, a tennis centre and a riding centre within easy reach. The town beach is tiny but there are plenty of others to the east.

Ferragudo ★★

On one side of the estuary of the river Arade is the big brash resort of Praia da Rocha; Ferragudo on the eastern side is a different place altogether. It still retains plenty of charm though, despite intense villa development on the outskirts. This pretty resort is tipped for stardom and is attracting a great deal of investment.

Local houses have all had a fresh lick of paint and, with their traditional chimneys, door knockers, tiling and flowers, look well cared for. The main square, with its bars and cafés, looks particularly smart. You can walk along the beach past the fishermen's huts, to the 17th-century fort which guards the entrance to the harbour.

Beyond the fort is **Praia Grande** (Big Beach), which is protected from the Atlantic waves by a sea wall and is one of the best beaches in the Algarve for windsurfing. You can hire equipment on the beach. If you continue onwards along the cliffs you will come to more isolated beaches: **Praia da Pintadinho**, **Praia dos Caneiros** and **Praia dos Torrados**.

SENHORA DA ROCHA TO BENAGIL WALK

This walk takes in some of the loveliest beaches in the Algarve. While the complete walk there and back is about 11km (7 miles) you may of course prefer to do only a part of the walk. Naturally you can start from the **Benagil** end as well. Begin the walk at the little church of **Senhora da Rocha** on the headland west of **Armação de Pêra**. The path is at first rough, as it leads up and down steep ravines running at right angles to the beaches. However, the going soon levels out to glorious clifftop views, and the chance of a swim as the path winds down to the beaches of Albandeira and Marinha.

INLAND
Silves ★★★

Silves is 13km (8 miles) north of Carvoeiro, and it is hard to believe that this sleepy country town in the foothills of the **Serra de Monchique** was once a rich and powerful city. One historian described it as 'stronger and ten times more remarkable than Lisbon'.

Believed to have been founded by the Phoenicians around 900BC, Silves has been settled for much longer, as **archaeological discoveries** in the area have produced many Bronze Age objects, and also evidence of Neolithic and Palaeolithic settlements. The 'Dog's Cistern' beneath the castle, which played an important role in the eventual capture of Silves by the Portuguese, is thought to be the pit of a copper mine first worked in Neolithic times.

Some historians believe that the walls and towers of the castle were built by the Romans and reinforced later. Certainly it appears to have been a town of some importance in the early centuries AD.

It was the Moors however who turned Silves into one of the richest cities in Europe. It was occupied by Arabs from the Yemen and was a city of mosques, bazaars, palaces and fine houses, likened to Baghdad. While Portugal as a whole was ruled from Seville, Silves (known as Xelb or Chelb) was the regional capital.

THE POETRY OF SILVES

These lines were written in the 11th century by the departing ruler of Silves, **Al Mutadid**.

At Silves, Abu Bakr, greet the dear places of my youth
Ask them whether they remember me, as I think they do.
Greet the Palace of Verandahs on behalf of a youth
Who is perpetually sighing for that palace,
The dwelling place of lions and white gazelles
Which at times seems a den and at others a seraglio.
How many nights have I not spent in its shade
In the sweet company of damsels with elegant waists
Some so white, others so dark that they caused in my soul
The effect of shining swords and black lances.

Below: *It is difficult to imagine that Silves was once one of the most splendid cities in Europe.*

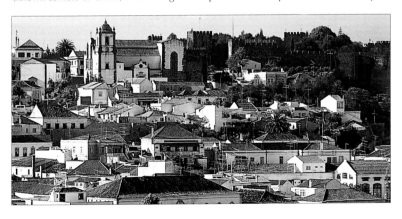

SOCCER CATALYST

It is just possible that the rarest cat in the world, the shy and beautiful Iberian lynx, is hanging on by a whisker in the hills of the northern Algarve. You can help them survive by supporting the Loulé-based football club Algarve United, an Anglo-Portuguese league team that donates a percentage of gate receipts to conservation group SOS Lynx and once had the colourful former England star, Paul Gascoigne, as its manager.

Below: *The charming main square at Silves is an ideal place to stop for a cold drink.*

'Silves has a strong wall, vegetable gardens and orchards,' wrote the Muslim geographer Idrisi in the 12th century. 'The residents drink water from a river that flows to the south. There are water mills on the river, a port and shipbuilding yards. Timber is very abundant on its hills and is exported to many regions. The town has a lovely appearance, beautiful buildings and very abundant markets. Its residents speak pure Arabic. They are verse makers, eloquent and well spoken.'

Silves's link with the sea is the river Arade, now silted up but then a vital commercial artery. Timber, cork, figs and oranges were exported to other parts of the Moors' empire. In the 9th century AD, Vikings swept down from the north and sailed up the Arade in their longboats, but the castle proved invincible that time around.

In 1189 **Sancho I** and a motley **Crusader** army regained control of Silves. The Arabs held out for months but ran out of water; the Christians had mined their way into the castle's underground galleries and isolated the water cisterns. The Crusaders reneged on the terms of surrender and murdered and looted at will.

Left: *The Moorish castle at Silves looks over the surrounding countryside.*

Silves was recaptured by the **Moors** two years later, but in 1249 fell again to the Portuguese under **Afonso III**. Silves declined over the next few centuries as first Lagos and then Faro grew to prominence.

Castle ★★

The best preserved castle in the Algarve, its turreted walls dominate the town and provide panoramic views over the countryside. The peaceful gardens within reveal no hint of the savage hand to hand fighting which once took place here, or indeed of the Moors' presence, aside from the deep well and the vaulted roof of the cistern which led by an underground passage to the Arade River. On the northern side some vestiges remain of the palace of **Aben Afan**, the last Moorish ruler of Silves. Open daily from 09:00–18:00.

A **beer festival** is held every July in Fabrica de Inglês (English Factory) near the river. This former cork processing complex has a museum devoted to the cork industry, lots of bars, cafés and fountains, and regular multimedia shows on summer evenings, featuring dancers, clowns and laser displays.

THE LEGEND OF SILVES

It is said that at midnight on the eve of **St John's Day** (Midsummer's Eve), an enchanted Moorish girl appears in the cistern of **Silves Castle**, sailing over the waters in a silver boat with golden oars and singing songs with strange melodies. She is awaiting her true prince who will say the magic words needed to break her spell. Enchanted Moorish girls figure heavily in Algarve folklore. Part siren, part witch, part innocent victim of sorcery, they embody the allure of the forbidden.

Above: Silves Cathedral has survived several major earthquakes and retains some of its Gothic features, despite extensive restoration over the centuries.

Archaeology Museum ★★

More informative than most, this modern museum has exhibits from prehistoric times onwards which include ceramics, jewellery, coins and pottery. The centrepiece is a Moorish cistern dating from the 12th century. Rua das Portas de Loulé 14; open 10:00–18:00; closed Mondays.

Sé de Santa Maria ★

This Gothic cathedral dates from the 13th century, and was the leading cathedral in the Algarve until the 16th century. Built on the site of a former mosque, it contains Crusader tombs. Open Monday–Saturday 09:00–13:00 and 14:30–18:00.

As you walk along the **Rua da Cruz da Palmeira** near the Arade River, you will see traces among the houses of the former Moorish walls, made of stone and mud, which once entirely encircled the city. The arched bridge over the Arade was built in the 13th century on the site of the original Roman bridge. If you stop for a cold drink or a snack at Café Rosa in the square next to the town hall, make sure you take a peek inside the café at the walls covered in blue and white *azulejos* and the elegant wrought iron furniture.

Near Silves

Some 10km (6 miles) northeast of Silves is the **Barragem do Arade**, one of the Algarve's major reservoirs. It's a lovely peaceful spot in the wooded hills ideal for a swim, walk or picnic. You can also hire canoes and motorboats.

Nearby, **São Bartolomeu de Messines** is a quiet country town, with an old parish church with characteristic twisting Manueline columns, surrounded by 17th- and 18th-century houses. Messines (as it is known locally) was the birthplace of one of the Algarve's most famous poets, **João de Deus** (1830–1896). His poems celebrate the beauty and simplicity of the countryside – still very much in evidence today.

Alte ★★

Known as the 'prettiest village in the Algarve', Alte is regularly featured on tour bus itineraries. Saturday is a particularly busy day, and a visit here can be combined with a shopping trip to Loulé's Gypsy Market, so if you're visiting independently you might like to schedule your visit for another day.

The village itself is very attractive, with spotless cottages displaying patios and balconies overflowing with flowers. The church too is flower filled, and embellished with beautiful blue and white *azulejos* from Seville and brightly coloured statues.

A five minute walk takes you to the fonte – a very popular picnic spot by the stream. The spring water here has a reputation as a cure-all. Some of the verses from local poet **Candido Guerreiro** (1871–1953) are displayed on tile panels on the banks. There are two restaurants here which run regular folklore evenings in summer. There's also a **May Day Festival** held here, and a **Folklore Festival** on the second Sunday in August. Alte is well known for its talented traditional singers, musicians and dancers.

EXPAT SCENE

There are currently around 50,000 British expats living in the Algarve and the number grows year after year. Many have set up English bars, restaurants and other tourism enterprises, others have married locals and yet more have chosen to retire in the sun. There are also significant numbers of Dutch and Scandinavian immigrants. The Alentejo has a growing number of German residents, many of whom have acquired farms. Most foreigners integrate well with the locals rather than remaining in expat enclaves.

Left: *Alte is considered one of the most appealing villages in the Algarve.*

Below: *Lagoa is the wine capital of the Algarve.*

Lagoa ★

Returning from Silves to the EN125, Lagoa is the town at the junction and is often bypassed by people hurrying back to the coast. It has no major sights, but is a pleasant place to wander around and admire the faded old buildings, many with pious religious *azulejos* on their walls.

The back streets have plenty of atmosphere, as do the little grocery shops which double as bars. If you arrive at midday you might well believe that someone had spirited all the inhabitants away; it is a much livelier place by early evening.

There's a large expat community living in the surrounding countryside here, and the town has excellent restaurants with prices cheaper than on the coast.

In front of the parish church with its Baroque façade are jacaranda trees, which in May and June are ablaze with vivid deep blue blossom. Here too is a war memorial which commemorates local men who died during the colonial wars from 1954–74. Lagoan blood has been spilt in Goa, Guinea, Mozambique and Angola.

Lagoa is the most important **wine producing** region of the Algarve. The vineyards which supply the *adegas* (wine shops) come from the area bounded by Silves, Albufeira and Loulé. The largest of the *adegas* is the

Lagoa Cooperative on the Portimão road, producing mainly red wine but also white and rosé. The reds are fruity and the whites reasonably dry, but both are high in alcohol content. Taste the wines before you buy at the Cooperative. The quality is not always as high as that of wines produced in other parts of Portugal.

Paderne ★★

Paderne is about 13km (8 miles) north of Albufeira, and is a typical country village, with some lovely crumbling dusty pink and faded coral façades on its old buildings. There's a handsome church, and the Central Café has a magnificent football table with the teams kitted out in the colours of top Lisbon clubs: Benfica (red) and Sporting CP (green).

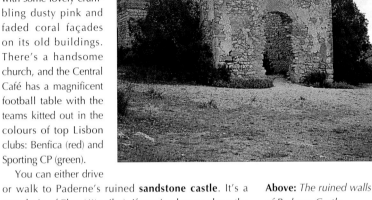

You can either drive or walk to Paderne's ruined **sandstone castle**. It's a round trip of 7km (4½ miles). If coming by car along the track, take the left-hand fork after the turn-off to Fonté and you'll be able to drive straight up to the castle.

Built by the Moors, it was conquered in 1249 by Dom Afonso III. Today only the outer walls remain to remind us of its former grandeur; within them are the ruins of a Gothic chapel. Look down from the castle at the high arched bridge spanning the river Quarteira, which is believed to date from Roman times. If you've mistakenly taken the right-hand fork don't despair – you can still get up to the castle, although it's a steepish scramble up the thyme- and sage-scented hill. Before you climb up, take a look at the abandoned mill by the stream with its elaborate dam, sluice gates and mill stone.

The tourist office in Albufeira can give you details of other walks around Paderne. These pass through interesting low intensity farmland where the hay is still gathered by hand. You pass through olive and orange groves, bright with poppies and bluebells in the spring; keep an eye out for orchids too. Only the buzz of traffic from the nearby motorway bridge disturbs the peace.

Above: *The ruined walls of Paderne Castle.*

COLONIAL LEGACY

Since the Moors arrived over a thousand years ago, African influence has become entrenched in Portuguese life. More recently, African colonial wars in Angola and Mozambique played a major role in the collapse of the Salazar regime. Conscripted army officers became sympathetic to the freedom fighters, and out of their ranks grew the MRA (Movimento das Forças Armadas), which toppled the government in the 1974 Revolution. Over half a million refugees returned to Portugal following colonial independence, bringing a new wave of African culture with them.

ALMONDS

The Moors were the first to cultivate almond trees in the Algarve. Bitter almonds can be distilled into liqueurs such as *amêndoa amarga*. Sweet almonds are eaten as appetizers, used in cooking, or mixed with egg yolk to form the basis of countless tooth-rotting but delectable desserts and confectionery. Marzipan cakes such as *morgado de figos do Algarve* (which has dried figs, chocolate, cinnamon and lemon peel) are an Algarve speciality and exceedingly sweet.

Below: *Even on a hot day there's a chill in the air at Alcantarilha's bone chapel.*

Guia ★

A mere 5km (3 miles) north of Albufeira at the junction with the EN125, Guia's claim to fame has less to do with its sights than its **cuisine**, although the magnificent cemetery just out of town on the Albufeira road is worth a visit. Guia is one of the places in the Algarve (the other is around Monchique) that specializes in **chicken *piri piri*** – barbecued chicken in hot chilli sauce. It's served with chips and salad, and is quite delicious and very cheap.

If you want to eat as the locals eat this is the place to come. Eating chicken *piri piri* in a large group of family or friends is a Friday and Saturday night ritual for many locals and expats. It's difficult to recommend a restaurant as they go in and out of fashion, and there are plenty of *piri piri* connoisseurs who debate the merits of one establishment over another.

Out of the dozen or more *piri piri* restaurants in Guia, most famous is **O Teodósio** – a huge, noisy place on the Algoz road with a fast turnover – which claims to be *Rei dos Frangos* (King of the Chickens). Regular customers come from as far away as Faro, and there's often a queue for tables in the evening. **O Alfredo** is just as good but quieter, while the long-established **O Viera** bills itself as the Famous House of Chicken. **Churrasqueira Ramires** also has an excellent reputation.

ALONG THE EN125

Porches is located 5km (3 miles) east of Lagoa, and is famous for its potteries, which can best be found along the main EN125 rather than in the village. **Olaria Pequena** has some lovely handpainted modern designs of fish and flowers that are sophisticated and tasteful, but by no means cheap. Porches also produces handpainted ceramics of high quality.

Alcantarilha is 5km (3 miles) east from Porches along the EN125 and is a quiet little town that the 20th century appears to have passed by. Alcantarilha is famous for its

bone chapel, which is around the side of the parish church. Apart from the crucifix, the entire interior is made up of the remains of approximately 1500 parishioners. Tightly packed skulls and bones catch the dim light from the doorway – it's eerie, and it's quite impossible to repress a shiver as you peer inside. The chapel is the only part of the parish church left standing after the Great Earthquake.

Above: *Water parks provide fun in the sun for all the family.*

Water Parks ★★
There are three in this stretch of the EN125. **Slide and Splash** is between Estômbar and Lagoa and has plenty of slides, from the gentle to the heart-stopping Kamikaze.

Aqualand is the largest water park in the Algarve and has over 1500m (4950ft) of chutes set in beautifully landscaped gardens. It's located halfway between Porches and Alcantarilha.

Zoomarine at Guia has elephant seals, dolphins and sea lions which perform tricks for tourists. It is billed as an educational experience for children but many visitors feel exploitation is a better description, particularly as the pools are too cramped for these large mammals. There are also swimming pools and a big wheel. The water park organizes free transportation from the main resorts in the area.

CHILDREN

The Algarve is a good place to take children on holiday. They are welcome in hotels and restaurants, and there are plenty of safe, sandy beaches and numerous sports and outdoor activities for them to enjoy. Some hotels organize children's events, while many have special children's swimming pools and play areas.

Central Algarve at a Glance

Spring and autumn see ideal temperatures for walking, golf and other outdoor activities. Winters are mild and often sunny but expect a few rainy days anytime between October and February. Summer can be hot but there is usually a refreshing breeze on the coast.

If coming to the central Algarve from Faro by public transport, there are regular express **buses** to Lagos, calling at Montechoro, Albufeira, Ferreiras, Armação de Pêra and Lagoa. Both Silves and Albufeira can be reached by **train**; the stations are a few kilometres outside the centre. If coming by train from Lisbon, change at Tunes junction near Albufeira for local services.

Local **buses** connect resorts up and down the coast and there are also regular services to Silves. The tourist office will have information and details. Hiring a **bicycle** is a good way of getting around but you may prefer to avoid the busy EN125.

Albufeira
LUXURY
Pine Cliffs, Pinhal do Cocelho, tel: 289 500 300, www.pinecliffs.com Since its

opening, the Pine Cliffs has gained a reputation as one of the Algarve's top hotels. Golf and various other sports are right on the doorstep.

MID-RANGE
Hotel Boa Vista, Rua Samora Barros 20, tel: 289 589 175, www.hotelboavista.pt Four-star hotel in a quiet but still relatively central location, with its own swimming pool.
Hotel Alisios, Avenida Infante d'Henrique 83, tel: 289 589 284, www.hotel alisios.com This four-star hotel has a heated pool as well as direct access to the beach. It also has great views.
Monte das Cortelhas, Caminho do Monte, Guia, tel: 289 561 487, www.montecortelhas.com Charming small hotel with flower-filled courtyards in quiet countryside.

BUDGET
Pensão Residencial Vila Recife, Rua Miguel Bombarda 12, tel: 289 586 747, fax: 289 587 182. Central location.
Parque de Campismo de Albufeira, tel: 289 587 629, www.algarve-gids.com This camp site is situated to the north of town, just off the road to the railway station.

Armação de Pêra
LUXURY
Vila Vita Parc, Alporchinos, tel: 282 310 100, www.vila

vitahotels.com This is one of the Algarve's top hotels, offering high standards of service as well as excellent accommodation.

MID-RANGE
Hotel Garbe, Avenida Marginal, tel: 282 320 260, www.thehotelgarbe.com This four-star, older-style traditional hotel has a loyal following. It also has direct access to the beach.
Casa Bela Moura, Alporchinhos, tel: 282 313 422, www.casabelamoura. com Small and delightfully stylish hotel in countryside, with heated pool and lovely gardens, 1.5km (1 mile) from the beach.

Carvoeiro
MID-RANGE
Hotel Carvoeiro Sol, Praia do Carvoeiro, tel: 282 320 260, www.thecarvoeirosol.com A medium-sized four-star hotel centrally located in the square overlooking beach. It has two small pools.
Hotel Cristal, Vale de Centeanes, tel: 282 358 601, www.cristalalgarve.com Clifftop location, four-star facilities, kitchenettes in rooms.

Silves
MID-RANGE
Hotel Colina dos Mouros, Pocinho Santo, tel: 282 440 420. Three-star hotel, pool and castle views.

Central Algarve at a Glance

Residencial Ponte Romana, Ponte Romana, tel: 282 443 275. Situated along the river, castle views and excellent country cooking.

Ferragudo
MID-RANGE
Vila Castelo, Angrinha, tel: 282 460 370, www.vila castelo.com Apartments, townhouses and villas to rent, modern facilities, with heated swimming pool.

BUDGET
Apartments Praia Grande, Rua da Hortinha 12, tel: 282 461 488. Reasonably priced apartments near the beach.

Alte
MID-RANGE
Alte Hotel, Montinho, tel: 289 478 523, www.alte hotel.com Small hotel above the village with heated pool and bus to the beach – the best of both worlds.

Vilamoura
LUXURY
Vilamoura Marinotel, tel: 289 303 303, fax: 289 303 345. A five-star hotel on the marina. Not much atmosphere but good sports facilities.

WHERE TO EAT

Albufeira
Restaurante Tipico A Ruina, Largo Cais Herculano, tel: 289 512 094. This seafood restaurant is very conveniently located on Fishermen's Beach,

and it affords lovely views from the roof terrace.
O Cabaz da Praia, Praca Miguel Bombarda, Albufeira, tel: 289 512 137. Michelin-starred fusion of French and Portuguese cuisine and great cliff-top views over the beach.

Ferragudo
Sueste, Rua da Ribiera, tel: 282 461 592. Dine on fresh fish right on the quayside.

Vilamoura
Akavit, Marina, tel: 289 380 712. This smart restaurant is particularly popular with the yacht set.

Carvoeiro
A Fonte, Escandhinas Vai Essar 4, tel: 282 356 707. Portuguese fare, charcoal-grilled fish and meat, pleasant outdoor terrace.

Armação de Pêra
Serol, Rua Portas do Mar, tel: 282 312 146. This is undoubtedly the best fish restaurant in town.

Silves
Restaurant Rui, Rua Comen-dador Vilarinho, tel: 282 442 682. This long-established seafood restaurant is some-thing of an institution in Silves. It is renowned for the good quality of its food and excel-lent value for money. Booking is advisable for dinner.
Café Ingles, tel: 282 442 585. Situated just beside the castle; meals and cakes are

served in the courtyard.

SPORTS AND ACTIVITIES
The **Montechoro Sports Club** (tel: 289 580 560, www. montechoroclub.com) offers tennis coaching, squash, a gym and health spa.

Horse Riding
Country Riding Centre, Silves, tel: 917 976 995. Hacks for all abilities.
Albufeira Riding Centre, Vale Navio, tel: 289 542 870. English-owned stables.

Scuba Diving
Indigo Divers, Rua Alexandre Herculano 16, Albufeira, tel: 289 587 013, www.indigo-divers.pt Padi-registered, offering beginners' courses that start safely in a swimming pool. Experienced divers can wreck-dive and explore caves and submerged cliffs.

USEFUL CONTACTS
Tourist Offices
Albufeira:
Rua 5 de Outubro, tel: 289 585 279.
Armação de Pera:
Avenida Marginal, tel: 282 312 145.
Carvoeiro:
Largo do Praia de Carvoeiro, tel: 282 357 728.
Quarteira:
Praça do Mar, tel: 289 389 209.
Silves:
Rua 25 de Abril, tel: 282 442 255.

4
Western Algarve

This is one of the most varied and rewarding parts of the Algarve, an area of great natural beauty unspoilt by overdevelopment. **Lagos** is, to many, the most interesting town to visit; steeped in history, but with a lively atmosphere, it combines fun with fascination. Neighbouring **Portimão** is famous for sardine lunches and shopping; the town itself is sedate but its southern suburb, **Praia da Rocha**, is the epitome of the brash holiday resort. These are few and far between in this part of the world. Tourism developments have been spreading west over recent years, but fortunately the developers appear to have run out of steam (or cash) beyond Portimão. There are many small resorts on the coast where you can get away from it all and enjoy a quiet holiday.

Although the **Barlavento** (windward) coast of the Algarve begins a few miles west of Faro, the characteristic landscape of weathered cliffs reaches a climax at **Sagres**. Here in the far west, the cliffs plunge 60m (200ft) down to the Atlantic.

The **beaches** up the western coast are quite magnificent and still in their natural state; the whole area is now protected by law, so any future development will be small-scale. The recent completion of the EN125 as far as Sagres has made access to the western coast much easier, but the coast as a whole still has a remote feel.

Turn inland to **Monchique** and you'll find lush woods and shady streams; here too is the highest peak in the Algarve at **Foia**, rising to 900m (3000ft).

DON'T MISS

★★★ Lagos: the history and style of the former capital.
★★★ West Coast: exploring the wild beaches.
★★ Portimão: eating sardines at the old harbour.
★★ Cruise: a cruise along the dramatic coastline.
★★ Sagres: take a trip to the end of the world.
★★ Monchique: get away from it all among the green hills around Monchique.

Opposite: *Weathered cliffs and dramatic rock formations make up the coastline of the western Algarve.*

Above: *Boat cruises to view the coastal scenery are easy to book in Portimão.*

PORTIMÃO ★★

After Faro, Portimão is the most important commercial centre in the Algarve. It's a busy town rather than a resort, but, perhaps because it makes few concessions to tourism, is a rewarding place to visit for the day.

The town is more amenable to sightseeing now the impressive new suspension bridge across the river Arade has been completed. This diverts through traffic away from the centre which used to be hopelessly congested, but is now much more pleasant for pedestrians.

If you're arriving by car, park near the old harbour and wander through the riverside gardens. After Olhão, Portimão is the leading fishing port in the Algarve. Watching the fish come in here used to be fascinating. Familiar and unfamiliar species of fish in wicker baskets would be thrown from the boats to waiting ice boxes on the quay. Now this all happens on the other side of the river.

You'll still see fishing smacks though, unloading sardines bound for the nearby restaurants. Also tied up at the quayside are smart sailing boats and big game cruisers. Portimão is the main centre for **leisure cruises** and big **game fishing** in the Algarve, and you can get information on these from the stalls by the quayside.

The cruise itineraries go either east to the spectacular coastal scenery of grottoes, cliffs and caves, as far as **Algar Seco past Carvoeiro**, or west beyond **Alvor**. A lunchtime stop at a cove only accessible from the sea, and a barbecue lunch followed by ample time to swim and snorkel, are common to all but the shortest cruises. You can also venture up the Arade River and visit Silves for the day, following in the wake of Phoenicians, Romans, Vikings and Moors. The vessel used is a shallow-keeled motorized canoe as the river is still too silted up for conventional boats, although there is talk of dredging it to allow more commercial traffic.

For a crash course in Portuguese history, you could do a lot worse than strolling around the little square of Largo 1 de Dezembro. The park benches here are backed by elaborate *azulejos* which depict key events in the country's evolution from 1143 to 1910. The square's name commemorates the end of Spanish sovereignty in 1640.

From here go up the main **shopping** streets, Rua Vasco da Gama and its continuation, Rua do Comércio. Casual fashions, bags, belts, shoes and handicrafts are all good buys here. See the old market and the interior *azulejos* of the **Church of the Colégio**, parts of which date back to the 15th century, in Praça da República. This impressive church stands on the highest part of town.

Don't leave without having a sardine lunch beneath the old bridge. There are plenty of restaurants to choose from, all offering similar menus and low prices. Traditional accompaniment is a salad, bread and *vinho verde*.

BIG GAME FISHING

You don't need to be an experienced fisherman to go on a big game fishing trip from Portimão, but it helps if you're a good sailor (particularly outside the summer when seas can be rough) and you're not too squeamish. You can still go as a spectator even if you don't intend to fish. The main quarry is shark – blue, copper and mako. Some of the big ones weigh in at over 100kg (220 lbs). It takes about two hours to get to shark territory. While waiting for the sharks to bite you can cast hand lines for bass, moray eels and rays.

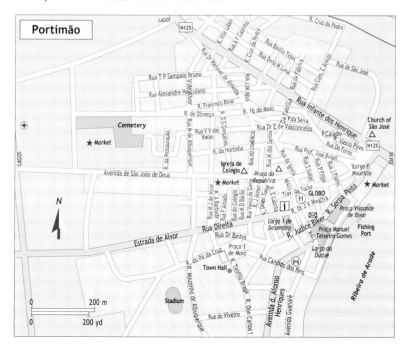

Right: *The beach at Praia da Rocha is one of the biggest in the Algarve and there's plenty of room for everyone.*

TRIP THROUGH TIME

To see the remains of the Roman **Vila Abicada**, drive west from Portimão on the EN125, turning left at the Figueira crossroads. Most of the finds from this 4th-century villa are now in the museum in Lagos, but some of the mosaics are still visible *in situ*. Return along the same road, passing through **Figueira** and continuing north to **Alcalar**. Here you'll find a megalithic tomb, the **Tumulos de Alcalar**. The chamber is visible and is thought to be at least 3000 years old.

DROPSY OR POISON?

King João II died in Alvor in 1495, after making an unsuccessful trip to take the waters at the spa of Monchique. His death is said to have been caused by poison rather than dropsy, and certainly he had many enemies in the Spanish court. Obsessed with the idea of finding Prester John, a legendary Christian king in Africa who the Portuguese believed could be roused against the Moors, he carried on the work of his great uncle, Henry the Navigator, by commissioning voyages along the African coast.

AROUND PORTIMÃO

To the west of Portimão and visible from the main road is an important wetland area, which bird lovers and conservationists have been fighting for years to preserve. But yet another marina is under way. Black-winged stilts, stone curlews, fan-tailed warblers and yellow wagtails breed (or used to breed) here; Caspian terns and ospreys are occasional winter visitors.

South of Portimão is **Praia da Rocha**, one of the first resorts in the Algarve to be developed. It's hard to believe, looking around the cheap souvenir shops, fast food joints and concrete apartment blocks, that back in the 1930s it was a genteel and elegant resort.

The prime attraction, both then and now, is the wonderful 2km (1¼ miles) beach. It is backed by sandstone cliffs, and interrupted by rock formations which have been sculpted into remarkable shapes, complete with tunnels and arches.

It's a good place to sleep off your sardine lunch, and is also the best centrally situated resort to try surfing, although the waves are higher further along the west coast. The sand looks as if it has been here for centuries, but in fact was brought from Portimão when the harbour was dredged. Along the clifftop promenade to the east is the 16th-century fortress of **Santa Catarina** built to defend the Arade estuary, but now housing an outdoor café with panoramic views.

Continuing on round the coast are more secluded and lovely beaches: **Vau**, **São João de Arens**, **Três Irmãos** and **Prainha** are the main coves.

Alvor ★

Located 8km (5 miles) west of Portimão on the estuary of the river of the same name, Alvor retains its fishing village charm. A favourite activity is sitting at the quayside in one of the good fish restaurants, and watching the catch being landed. Prawns go virtually straight from the boat to the charcoal grill.

Alvor became an important port during the Moorish occupation and once had its own castle, which was destroyed by the earthquake in 1755. The village itself is a maze of cobbled streets, and the portal of the parish church displays its Manueline influences with a round arch, delicate fretwork and the use of abstract floral motifs. Dedicated to the Holy Saviour, it dates from the 16th century but was rebuilt after the earthquake. Most holiday accommodation is near the town beach 1km (⅔ mile) away. Further east, the coastline breaks into a series of rocky coves and sandstone cliffs – good for walks and snorkelling.

Opposite: *The façade of Santo António belies its sumptuous interior.*
Below: *This lovely beach is close to Lagos's museum of the Great Discoveries.*

LAGOS ★★★

Lagos has all the ingredients for a successful holiday: plenty of sights, a friendly atmosphere, good restaurants, trendy bars and excellent beaches. Its easy-going atmosphere attracts students and youngsters from all over Europe during the summer, and *alfresco* concerts, jam sessions and pavement markets become part of the scene.

Lagos has a superb natural harbour and a long history. The Phoenicians, Carthaginians, Romans and Moors all settled here, and it was the capital of the Algarve from 1576–1765. Lagos was Henry the Navigator's base port for African trade during the age of the Great Discoveries in the 15th century. Under his patronage a Lagos captain, Gil Eanes, rounded Cape Bojador in West Africa.

This was not as simple as it sounds. Apart from the legends of sea monsters and demons, the waters were known to the Arabs as the Green Sea of Darkness, because of the tricky combination of unfavourable winds, violent waves and strong currents which had swallowed many a vessel. Once this physical and psychological barrier was overcome, Africa and its store of gold, ivory and slaves was ripe for the taking.

A good place to start your exploration of Lagos is in front of the statue of **Prince Henry** in the Praça da República by the waterfront. Cross the road and turn right to the old 17th-century fort, **Ponta da Bandeira**, which guarded the harbour. This is now an interesting museum dedicated to the Great Discoveries.

Inside are fascinating reproductions of old maps, diagrams and pictures of sailing ships, and a chronological history of the growth of Portugal's great maritime empire.

Crossing back to the square, look out for the small arcade at the top right-hand corner. This was Europe's first **slave market**, where many hundreds of thousands of captives were bought and sold for a few *reals*. It now enjoys a happier reincarnation as an art gallery.

Church of Santo António ★★

Leave the square by Rua de São Gonçalo; on your left is the Santo António church. Plain on the outside, the interior is a fantasia of gold baroque woodwork. Known as the **Golden Chapel**, it is an excellent example of *igreja toda de ouro* (church interior covered in gilded woodwork). The *azulejo* panels on the walls depict scenes from the life of Saint Anthony.

Municipal Museum ★

Exhibits at the museum next door include archaeological finds, a 17th-century mobile altar, agricultural implements, model peasants in costume, preserved animal foetuses and fish, old books and a model of an imaginary Algarve village. Museum and church are open 09:00–12:30 and 14:00–17:00 Tuesday–Sunday.

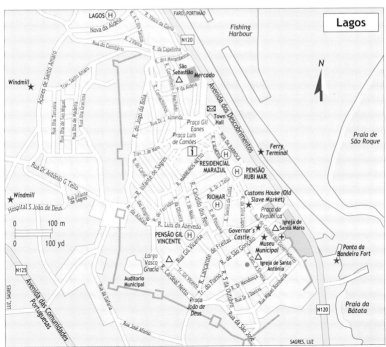

SLAVERY

Henry the Navigator found African slaves a useful way of financing his voyages. At first forcibly abducted from their west coast villages, they were later obtained with help from local chiefs, who found the trade a profitable way to deal with captives from inter-tribal warfare. The miserable trade grew as other European nations did the same and, at its peak in the 18th century, seven to ten million slaves were shipped out of Africa. The **Marquês de Pombal** emancipated Portuguese slaves in 1773, but it took almost a century for slave trading to be finally abolished.

PARQUE NATURAL DO SUDOESTE ALENTEJANO E COSTA VICENTINA

This new nature park runs from Burgau up the western Algarve and Alentejo coast. It is effectively a narrow coastal strip made up of cliffs, estuaries, beaches, marshes and hills containing many rare plants, and is also an important migratory stop for birds. Look out for resident ospreys and storks. The park's headquarters are over the border in the Alentejo at Odemira (tel: 283 227 35); there is also an office in Aljezer (tel: 282 998 673).

Right: *Shopping is fun in Lagos and there are many stylish boutiques.*

Cross to the Rua da Silva Lopes and continue into the pedestrianized Rua 25 de Abril. This is where you'll find many of Lagos's best **restaurants**. There are also plenty of boutiques should your beach wardrobe need refreshing.

In Praça Gil Eanes you will see a modern statue which has been variously described as a flowerpot man, a mod spaceman and a sci-fi alien. In fact it is supposed to be **Dom Sebastião**, who gained the throne in 1568, and ten years later launched a disastrous crusade to Morocco (*see* pages 15–16). You can see the window from where he is said to have addressed his troops in the **Church of the Misericórdia** in the Praça da República.

Continuing down the Rua das Portas de Portugal you'll pass the well-stocked **fish market** on your left; there are plenty of inviting cafés here with views over the fishing harbour. Stop for a coffee and perhaps one of the many delectable cakes for which Lagos is famous. There are different varieties made from almonds, eggs, marzipan or figs.

Around 8km (5 miles) north of town on the road to Aljezur, **Lagos Zoo** is a small, shady park featuring monkeys, exotic birds and a petting zoo.

WEST ALONG THE COAST

Travelling west along the coast from Lagos, the first beach resort visitors will encounter is **Dona Ana**, which is now virtually a satellite of Lagos. It gets rather crowded in summer, but is very pretty with its weathered cliffs, grottoes and stacks. Visitors are able to walk from here to Ponta da Piedade; from the lighthouse you have wonderful views all the way to Carvoeiro in the east and to Sagres in the far west.

Luz, 10km (6 miles) west of Lagos, has a good-sized sandy beach with sailing, windsurfing, water-skiing and diving all on tap. It's still a relatively peaceful place for a holiday, but is the fastest-developing package tourism resort on this stretch of coast, and apartments and villas are spreading in all directions.

As you approach **Burgau** a blast of fantasy Moorish architecture alerts you to the fact that this is another up and coming resort. But it's prettier than many, and still has a fair amount of its original fishing village charm, with its red-roofed cottages and cobbled streets. Heavy seas have washed away most of the sand from the town beach, but there are some alternatives round the point to the west. The English-run Burgau Sports Centre offers tennis, squash, volleyball and football, as well as a swimming pool.

Salema is still very much a working fishing village. Fishermen mend their nets on the long sandy beach and it has managed to maintain an authentic rustic look. But a couple of big apartment blocks have gone up and time share touts are working the area. You can rent windsurfers and pedaloes on the beach.

Further west, take the road south of Raposeira for some secluded beaches: **Zaival**, **Ingrina**, **Barranco** and **João Vaz** – the latter a favourite spot for those in pursuit of an all-over tan.

Above: *The coastline near Salema alternates between coves and rocky cliffs.*

OFF THE BEATEN TRACK

Pony trekking is an excellent way of seeing the more remote areas. There are riding schools throughout the region that cater for novices and experts. You could hire a **four-wheel-drive** to explore the rough mountain roads, but go on a **jeep safari** to relax and let others take the wheel. There are numerous **cruises** to offshore islands, caves and picturesque beaches, and you can take a short **flight** for a bird's-eye view of the coast.

SEA BATTLES

This part of the coast has seen plenty of action. **Christopher Columbus** was shipwrecked off **Cape St Vincent** in 1476 en route from Genoa to England. His ship was attacked by pirates, but he managed to escape by swimming an incredible 10km (6 miles) to shore.

Francis Drake, one of Elizabeth I's most trusted naval commanders, was despatched to 'singe the King of Spain's beard' in 1587. At the time, Spain ruled Portugal and was gathering an armada to sail against England. Drake destroyed a fleet of Spanish ships in **Cádiz**, and on his return journey sacked **Vila do Infante**. The French defeated a British fleet here in 1693, while the British were victorious here against the Spaniards in 1797.

SAGRES ★★

The windswept Sagres peninsula, with its arid scrubby vegetation and dramatic cliffs, is a complete contrast to the rest of the Algarve. It's not pretty enough for most mainstream tourists and, unlike the sheltered south coast, the weather can be windy for days on end. But it has a devoted following among young international travellers.

They come to enjoy the wild beaches and stay either at the camp site, in cheap pensions or in the many rooms to rent in private houses. The evening scene revolves around animated talk in half a dozen different languages in the bars around the square in front of Café Conchina. One of the main topics of conversation is how expensive everything has become, not like in the good old days!

Cabo de São Vicente is the southwestern-most point of continental Europe and has a real end of the world feel. To the Phoenicians, Greeks, Carthaginians and Romans this is what it was; beyond the cape lay the great unknown.

The lighthouse here is one of the most powerful in Europe, and is said to be visible from 90km (55 miles) out to sea. Just outside it, stalls do a roaring trade, selling thick-knit fishermen's sweaters to shivering day trippers. To avoid paying over the odds, pack an extra jumper.

Left and opposite: *Cabo de São Vicente marks the most southwesterly point of Europe.*

The cliff tops between the cape and Sagres are home to a wide variety of **wild flowers**. In spring there are colourful clumps of thrift, blue pimpernels and miniature daffodils. Migrating **sea birds** fly over the cape on their way to and from the Mediterranean, between September and November and January to March.

If you are visiting at these times of year you can expect to see great flocks of gannets, big white sea birds with black-tipped wings, which breed in Britain but winter in the Mediterranean. Cabo de São Vicente is their cue to make a 90° turn and fly due east instead of south. Land birds include choughs, rock doves, and the occasional rare peregrine falcon.

HOW CABO DE SÃO VICENTE ACQUIRED ITS NAME

Cape St Vincent supposedly gets its name from a Spanish priest who was martyred in the 4th century. His remains were washed ashore at the **promontorium sacrum**, or Sacred Cape as it was called by the Romans. A church was built on the spot, watched over by 10 ravens. When St Vincent's remains were taken to Lisbon in the 12th century the ravens went too, maintaining their vigil from the ship's rigging. By contrast you will be lucky to spot a raven today; they have been shot and poisoned almost to extinction.

Above: *Some historians believe the Compass Rose was used to train the early navigators.*

BARING IT ALL

Nudity is no longer the shocker it was a few years ago, but theoretically the police can still prosecute. The rule of thumb appears to be that nude sunbathing is acceptable on remote beaches not accessible by car, and so unlikely to have much family custom. Nudity is quite widespread in the Sagres peninsula and the west coast. Walk for a mile or so from the nearest parking spot if in any doubt, and see how much your fellow sunbathers are baring. Topless sunbathing on most Algarve beaches is commonplace nowadays.

The walls of the **Fortaleza** (fortress) rise up on the promontory at the southern tip of the Sagres peninsula. This is where Henry the Navigator is said to have founded the **Vila do Infante**, his famous school of navigation, around 1420, but the actual location is a mystery. Sir Francis Drake razed part of it in 1587 when Portugal was under Spanish occupation, and the 1755 earthquake destroyed the rest.

It was in Sagres that Henry the Navigator gathered the best minds in Europe to correlate existing geographical knowledge, prepare new maps and advance navigational science. This was where shipbuilders pored over plans for the caravel, the innovative sailing ship which was to be the key to Portugal's marine domination of the globe.

Within the fortress walls are a small museum, an old church, and a giant compass scratched out on stone, which was only discovered in 1928 beneath the floor of a church. Historians are divided as to whether or not it dates from Henry's time.

The great Atlantic rollers pounding the peninsula's beaches act as a magnet for surfers; **Tonel**, to the west of Sagres, usually has reliable waves. The more sheltered **Praia do Martinhal** to the east and **Praia de Beliche** between Sagres and Cabo de São Vicente are, however, more attractive to swimmers.

MONCHIQUE

A day trip up into the beautiful shady hills makes for a refreshing change of scenery, particularly on a blisteringly hot summer's day. The woods which cloak the Serra de Monchique are made up of chestnut, pine, eucalyptus and cork oak trees; oleanders and arbutus provide splashes of colour.

If you see smoke rising from a field or woodland clearing, it is a sign that charcoal burners are at work. Branches are covered with earth and left to smoulder for a week. The result is a light, easy burning charcoal, which is used to grill sardines and other fish throughout the Algarve.

Caldas de Monchique ★★

The waters of this little spa town have been famous since Roman times for their curative properties. The modern treatment centre offers therapy for respiratory, rheumatic and intestinal disorders, and the modern spa has various hydrotherapies and massage. If visiting in summer, arrive early before the tourist coaches to savour the tranquility. Picnic by the stream or have lunch at the Restaurante Central in the shady square. Good buys in the shops include handicrafts and locally produced honey and *medronho*.

GETTING HIGH

Drive up to the highest peak in the Algarve at **Foia** and enjoy the panoramic views. The poet **Robert Southey** claimed you could see the hills of far-away **Sintra** north of Lisbon from here. For a view which is almost equally good, but may be admired from much lovelier surroundings, you can walk up to the summit of **Picota**, which is on the opposite side of the **Serra de Monchique** valley to Foia. It's a 9km (5½-mile) round trip but the gradient is not too tough.

Below: *The hillside terraces near Monchique were probably laid down over 1000 years ago by the Moors.*

Monchique ★★

On your way here stop at the lay-by for a panoramic
view of Caldas, and perhaps buy sweet oranges and
succulent dried figs from the handful of stalls alongside the road. Look out for the man with his handsome
dressage-trained donkey that performs showy half-
passes and poses for photographs.

Monchique is a market town which holds a big livestock fair on the third Friday of every month. The cobbled
streets are lined with old houses. Be sure not to miss the
elaborate Manueline doorway of the parish church in Rua
da Igreja, with its columns carved to resemble nautical
ropes and knots. You can walk up to the ruined **Convento
da Nossa Senhora do Desterro** above the town for lovely
views of the surrounding hills and woods.

Back in town, glance inside the Restaurant Central in
Rua da Igreja. The interior is festooned with hundreds
of scribbled messages on business cards, photographs,
bus passes, museum tickets and anything else to hand.
All attest to how they have had the meal of their lives.
Unfortunately, these days the food is mediocre and
prices on the high side.

Around Monchique

One of the loveliest drives in the Algarve is across the hills from Monchique to **Aljezur**. It runs through oak woods, the clearings dappled with sunlight and wild flowers. Just outside Aljezur is a more cultivated area where the old medieval system of strip farming is still practised. Strip farming is used for crop rotation; the narrow plots here are still worked by hand and ditches are used for irrigation. Sleek chestnut-hued cattle graze between the vegetable plots and tiny hay fields. At Aljezur, you can drive all the way up to the ruined sandstone castle and enjoy the view. It was originally built by the Moors in the 10th century.

CHRISTOPHER COLUMBUS

There is a story that Columbus was Portuguese. Certainly he was married to a Portuguese and used Portuguese cartography. Some scholars believe he was born, not in Genoa, but the small Alentejo town of **Cuba**. Another theory is that he was a Portuguese spy at the Spanish court, placed there to divert the expansionist Spaniards westwards, while the Portuguese planned to discover an eastern sea route to India and the riches of the Orient. Whatever the truth, the Portuguese feel the world has forgotten about their small country's tremendous contributions to the modern world.

Opposite: *View of Monchique from the Convento da Nossa Senhora do Desterro.*
Left: *Monchique's 16th-century parish church is a fine example of the eclectic Manueline style.*

WEST COAST BEACHES

Virtually the entire west coast as far north as the estuary of the **Rio Sado** south of Lisbon is composed of beaches. **Odeceixe**, 17km (10½ miles) north of Aljezur, marks the boundary between the Algarve and the Alentejo. North of this there is little organized holiday accommodation, but camping is a good alternative. **Vila Nova de Milfontes** is an exception. Popular with holiday-makers from Lisbon and the Alentejo, the old town has plenty of atmosphere and there are water sports on the beach. Further north, **Porto Covo** is a fishing village with rooms to rent. You can hire a boat here and visit its offshore island which contains the ruins of a 17th-century fort.

WEST COAST BEACHES ★★★

The whole west coast of the Algarve, from Cabo de São Vicente to Odeceixe, consists of wild and beautiful beaches and cliffs, reached by tracks and minor roads running west from the main road. At the southern end, **Praia do Amado** and **Praia do Castelo** have better road access than most. Surfers come from all over Europe to ride the rollers.

If you visit on a fine, still day you will probably think you have discovered paradise, but be careful when swimming, as the waves are rough and some of the beaches have a strong undertow. It can sometimes be windy here for days on end, but if you want to get back to nature and enjoy the fabulous scenery without commercial trappings and crowds, you will be in your element.

Driving north you will pass through a strange landscape – wild, melancholic and evocative. The little rounded hills are mirrored by stunted umbrella pines – both look like children's drawings. At **Carrapateira**, huge cacti flourish among the dunes and are used by the villagers as windbreaks for their tiny vegetable plots. The beach here is enormous, and you can walk either south along the top of the towering cliffs or north around the headland, to discover yet another fabulous beach: **Praia da Bordeira**.

The nearest beach to Aljezur is **Arrifana**, and to reach it you pass through windswept moor, yellow with broom flowers in spring. The beach is beautiful, backed by imposing cliffs and good for surfing. There are a handful of restaurants and a few simple places to stay, but most visitors stay at one of three camp sites.

Below: *The gorgeous beach at Arrifana is typical of the west coast.*

Western Algarve at a Glance

BEST TIMES TO VISIT

Spring and autumn are ideal. Winters are mild and sunny but expect a few rainy days from October to February. Summer can be hot but there is usually a breeze on the coast.

GETTING THERE

Train or express **coach** from Faro to Portimão or Lagos.

GETTING AROUND

Regular buses from Lagos to Luz, Burgau, Salema, Sagres and Aljezur, and from Portimão to Silves and Monchique.

WHERE TO STAY

Portimão
BUDGET
Residencial O Patio, Rua Dr João Vitorino Mealha 3, tel: 282 424 288. Central and very reasonably priced.

Praia da Rocha
MID-RANGE
Hotel Bela Vista, tel: 282 450 480. Four-star accommodation in old mansion.

Alvor
LUXURY
Le Meridien Penina Golf Hotel, Montes de Alvor, tel: 282 420 200, www.starwood hotels.com Fine golf resort.

Lagos
MID-RANGE
Sol e Praia, tel: 282 762 026. Right on the Dona Ana beach, with pool and gym.
Villa Marazul, Rua da Misercordia, tel: 282 760 261,

www.sonelhotels.com Situated on the outskirts of town, pools, modern studios.
Hotel Riomar, Rua Cândido dos Reis 83, tel: 282 770 130, fax: 282 763 927. Modern and very central.

BUDGET
Residencial Marazul, Rua 25 de Abril 13, tel: 282 770 230, fax: 282 769 960. This small hotel is friendly and very centrally located.

Salema
MID-RANGE
Estalagem Infante do Mar, tel: 282 690 100. Pretty inn; tiled floors and sea views.
Hotel Residencial Salema, Rua 28 de Janeiro, tel: 282 695 328. Overlooking the harbour.

Sagres
MID-RANGE
Pensão Residencia Dom Henrique, tel: 282 620 003. Small, modern, with sea views from balconies and terrace.
Casa Sagres, Praça da Republica, tel: 282 624 358. Atlantic views, pretty patio.

CAMP SITES
Alvor: 282 459 178. **Lagos:** Trinidade, tel: 282 763 893. **Luz:** Valverde, tel: 282 789 211; Espiche, tel: 282 789 265. **Salema:** Quinta dos Carricos, tel: 282 695 201. **Zavial:** Ingrina, tel: 282 639 242. **Sagres:** tel: 282 624 371. **Aljezur:** Serrão, tel: 282

990 220; São Miguel, tel: 282 947 145; Camping Vale de Telha, tel: 282 998 444.

WHERE TO EAT

Vilha Velha, Sagres, tel: 282 624 788. New take on trad Portuguese cooking.
A Lagosteira, Rua 1 de Maio 2, Lagos, tel: 282 762 486. Up-market restaurant where prawns, lobster and cataplana are the house specials.
Restaurante Piri Piri, 15 Rua Lima Leitao, Lagos, tel: 282 763 803. Popular traditional restaurant.
Mullens, Rua Candido dos Reis 86, Lagos. Lively bar with good food and music.

USEFUL CONTACTS

Tourist Offices
Aljezur: Largo do Mercado, tel: 282 998 229.
Lagos: Largo Marquês de Pombal, tel: 282 763 031.
Portimão: Cais do Comercio, tel: 282 470 556.
Praia da Rocha: Rua Tomas Cabreira, tel: 282 419 132.
Tiffany's Riding Centre, Vale Grifo, Almadena, Lagos, tel: 282 697 395. English-run; ponies for children, instruction, beach rides, hacking.
Turinfo, Praca de Republica, Sagres, tel: 282 620 003. Mountain biking, jeep safaris, fishing trips.
Bom Dia, Lagos, tel: 282 087 587; schooner cruises.
Horizonte, Salema Beach Club, tel: 282 695 920; jeep safaris into the coastal Natural Park plus other excursions.

5
Eastern Algarve

The Eastern Algarve stretches from Olhão to Vila Real de Santo António on the Spanish border and, apart from the wild western beaches, this is the least commercialized coastal area in the Algarve. Only a few miles inland you feel that you are in really remote countryside.

There are exceptions of course, and **Monte Gordo** in the extreme east is one of them; it is not the most attractive of resorts. It is visible from the atmospheric castle at **Castro Marim**, which once belonged to the mysterious Knights Templar.

Tavira and **Olhão** both vie for the title of most authentic south coast town among long-time Algarve fans. You can explore the lush and peaceful **Guadiana River** which forms the border between Portugal and Spain, by boat or car, and discover empty sandy beaches on the offshore islands.

The eastern half of the Algarve is known as the **Sotavento**, or leeward side. What it lacks in dramatic cliff scenery is made up for by an unusual landscape of lagoons, sand spits and islands. All the coastline here is part of the **Ria Formosa Nature Reserve**. One bonus for swimmers is that the water is a few degrees warmer here than in the more exposed west. Package tourism in the area is confined to just three resorts: **Monte Gordo** and the much smaller **Cabanas** and **Manta Rota**. By contrast, the offshore islands of **Ilha da Armona**, **Ilha da Culatra** and **Ilha da Fuzeta** have gained a word-of-mouth reputation among young travellers as 'cool' places to camp.

DON'T MISS

★★★ **Barrier Islands:** take a boat trip to these islands.
★★ **Exploring:** the wild hill country behind the coast.
★★ **Castro Marim:** a visit to the atmospheric castle.
★★ **Boat trip:** by boat up the Guadiana River to Alcoutim.
★★ **Olhão:** try the very good fresh seafood.

Opposite: *Pause for a while in one of Tavira's many lovely little parks.*

EPIC VOYAGE

The fishermen of Olhão have long held the reputation for being the most daring in the Algarve. But their finest hour came in 1808, when an intrepid crew sailed a small boat across the Atlantic to Rio de Janeiro – without navigational aids – to deliver to the exiled **King João II** the good news that Napoleon's troops had retreated from Portugal. As a reward, Olhão was given the status of a town and money was invested in the fishing industry, laying the foundations for a prosperous future.

Below: *Offerings at the tiny chapel of Nossa Senhora dos Aflitos.*

OLHÃO ★★

Olhão is 10km (6 miles) east of Faro, and as you drive through its northern suburbs from the EN125 and see the shabby apartment blocks, tyre workshops and advertising hoardings, you would never guess what a pleasant town lies in store just a few minutes away. Head for the seafront and park by the large fish and vegetable markets; take a look inside them if you want to whet your appetite for lunch. Olhão has the reputation as being the best town in the Algarve in which to enjoy the freshest of **fresh seafood**. The fish landed here is sold throughout Portugal, but plenty finds its way to local restaurants.

In the **Jardim Pescador Olhanense**, pleasant gardens just west of the markets, admire the *azulejo*-backed benches which depict key events in Olhão's history, then head inland to the **Fishermen's Quarter**. Start in the small square just opposite the gap between the two markets, turn right, and meander up and down the maze of tiny cobbled lanes. Most guidebooks rave about the cubist architecture of the houses here; this is an exaggeration, but certainly there is a hint of a North African kasbah here, a legacy of the local fishermen's voyages south to Morocco in search of tuna.

In the tiny Rua Santo Estevão (a right turn off the Rua Marquês de Pombal), listen for the sound of soulful *fado* guitar coming from no. 31. Mário Caleça often takes time off from his cobbler's shop next door to serenade his neighbours and passers by.

You will find the tourist office slightly northwest of here, off the

pedestrianized Rua do Comércio which is full of shops and boutiques. Continue north to the large Baroque 17th-century parish church, the **Igreja da Nossa Senhora do Rosário**, at the end of the main thoroughfare, the Avenida da República. At the back of the church is a tiny open chapel, the **Nossa Senhora dos Aflitos**. Here the wives of fishermen used to pray to the Virgin Mary for the safety of their menfolk out at sea. In a glass case are wax legs, arms and heads – votive offerings left by those in search of cures for ailments. The wax dolls have been left by women wanting to bear children.

If lunch beckons, you'll find a good choice of restaurants down on the seafront. Olhão is one of the least expensive places in the Algarve to enjoy fresh giant prawns, although sadly even here they can't be called cheap. They are, however, a delicious treat.

On your way out of town, drive to the eastern end of the seafront, and turn left just past the ferry terminal from which you can catch boats to the islands. Drive up past the port, where the numerous fishing boats of all sizes, and the number of repair workshops, testify to the continuing importance of the fishing industry.

Above: *Fishing is still a way of life in Olhão.*

OLHÃO BEACHES

There are eight boats a day in summer (Jun–Sep) from Olhão to the islands of **Armona** and **Culatra**, glorified sand bars which many rank as the best beaches in Portugal. In off-peak season there are two boats a day. It's just a 15-minute sail to **Armona**. The water on the land side where the ferry docks is warm and sheltered; this is where you find beach bars and restaurants. Walk across the island to the Atlantic side to get away from the crowds. **Ilha da Culatra** is yet more peaceful – it takes 45 minutes to get there, so pack a picnic. On both islands you can sunbathe nude among the dunes if you find a secluded spot.

SALT PANS

The *salinas* (salt pans) of the **Ria Formosa** produce half of Portugal's salt output. Salt has been harvested in the Algarve for over 2000 years. Seawater is directed into evaporation pans, each the size of a football pitch. After impurities have dropped to the bottom the water is moved to evaporation pans where, under the influence of the strong sun, the remaining water evaporates leaving slushy salt crystals. These are raked out and left to dry. Former pans are excellent habitats for birds.

Opposite: *The Algarve Water Dog.*
Below: *The Ria Formosa National Park.*

RIA FORMOSA NATURE RESERVE ★★

Most visitors' first view of the Algarve is the panorama of salt pans, marshes, barrier islands and lagoons which come into view as the aircraft banks before landing at Faro airport. For the vast majority heading for holiday beaches, this is also their last view of one of the most important wetland areas in Europe.

The Nature Reserve covers an area of 18,400ha (45,466 acres), and stretches along the coast, from **Quinta do Lago** west of Faro, all the way to **Manta Rota**. The interpretative centre just to the east of Olhão will provide you with a fascinating introduction to the unique ecology of the area, and will also make individual exploration much more meaningful.

In the centre itself you will get a general orientation of the park. There are large **aquariums** containing some of the key fish and molluscs to be found in the lagoons, from clams to a big octopus and fearsome-looking moray eels which lurk in large pots at the bottom of the tank.

Also on display is a sad exhibition of illegal bird traps and fishing nets collected by the conservationists. Much of the centre's work is aimed at educating children to preserve wildlife and the environment. Portuguese adults appear to be regarded as a lost cause.

Then go on a self-guided **walking tour** around this corner of the park, and take a closer look at some salt pans and an old tuna fishing boat. There is a fascinating tide mill, in perfect working order, which was used for grinding corn. It is the only one left along this stretch of coast – there were formerly 29.

At the **bird hide** you can see storks nesting along with ducks, waders and tortoises, while further along is a reconstruction of a typical farmhouse and an archaeological dig. A Roman salt fish factory has been discovered here. Using their feet, sailors crushed dried mackerel and tuna with oil and herbs to make garum, which was then stored in amphorae – earthenware pots which are on display. The garum was an important source of protein on long sea voyages.

You'll probably hear the next attraction before you see it. The **Algarve Water Dogs** bred here once worked with fishermen, but their alert nature, size and loud bark is giving the breed renewed popular appeal as guard dogs.

Returning to the interpretation centre you walk through a sandy area shaded by umbrella pines. This is a **chameleon** habitat. These delightful lizards can only be found in the more sheltered coastal regions of the Algarve from Albufeira to Monte Gordo. The only other place in Europe you can find them is in southern Spain. Keep an eye on the tree tops for an eagle, which was released from the bird recovery centre in the reserve, but liked the wood (and the bountiful resident mouse population) so much he stayed. The bird clinic is not open to the public, but usually contains a mix of injured falcons, eagles, vultures and owls which have been brought in for treatment. It is one of only three in the whole of Portugal.

Open 09:00–12:00 and 14:00–17:00 Mon–Fri. Turn right, following the signs for Quinta do Marim just past the last houses of Olhão on the EN125 east to Tavira.

ALGARVE WATER DOG

This dog, standing about 60cm (24in) at the shoulder, is one of the earliest known breeds in the world and is largely unchanged from the 16th century. It was also one of the rarest breeds in the mid-1970s, as rich breeders fleeing the country killed their dogs rather than find new homes for them. Town councils in dispute with fishermen also systematically poisoned them. Now their friendly and intelligent nature is finding them new roles as pets, and also as sniffer dogs employed by customs officers. They have webbed feet, can dive well, and used to help fishermen by relaying messages between boats, driving shoals of fish into nets, guarding the catch and even saving sailors from drowning.

TAVIRA BEACH

Tavira's beach, like those of Olhão, lies on an offshore island. The ferry terminal is about 2km (1¼ miles) from the centre of town, past the markets and through the salt pans, and buses depart from the Praça da República. There are several boat services daily to the long and lovely beaches. Hang out with the crowds on the inshore side with its rickety beach bars, or head to the seaward side if you want to be alone.

Opposite: *Banana plants outside the Convento de Santo António add an exotic flavour.*

TAVIRA ★★

An elegant little town, Tavira lies 20km (12½ miles) northeast of Olhão, and over the years it has lost very little of its low key charm. The foundations of the stone arched bridge date back to Roman times. The town developed during the Moorish occupation, and by the 15th century was one of the largest and most important ports in the Algarve, achieving city status in 1504. The gradual silting up of the Gilão River led to a decline in trade however, and tuna fishing took over as the main commercial activity. Since the 1970s the remaining tuna, their stocks already depleted, have changed their migratory routes south and westwards down the Moroccan coast. Storks now nest on the chimneys of abandoned canneries. However, Tavira is still an important fishing port.

Tavira was also badly damaged in the Great Earthquake and most of its fine buildings date from the late 18th century. The main square, the Praça da República, is on the west bank of the river. Enjoy a coffee in one of the open-air cafés in the gardens by

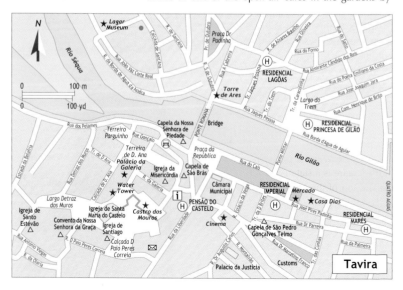

the river, and then head for the castle via the tourist office next to the town hall. Go up the quaint cobbled street opposite, the Rua da Galeria, and you'll pass the 16th-century Renaissance **Church of the Misericórdia**.

Pause to admire the interesting doorway with its carved heads, including an old fertility symbol, the Green Man, with vines and vegetation trailing from his mouth. Among the saints and angels are sea horses, mermen and what looks very like a rock guitarist, complete with leads coming from his guitar.

Of the castle, originally a Moorish fort rebuilt by Dom Dinis in the 13th century, only the walls remain. There's a pretty garden within the walls, and good views over the town and surrounding salt pans.

Next to the castle walls is the large **Church of Santa Maria do Castelo**, originally built on the site of a former mosque in the 13th century, but rebuilt after the earthquake. Like most of Tavira's 27 churches, it is only open for services. It contains the tomb of Dom Paio Peres Correia, who took Tavira from the Moors in 1224. The church with a striking interior is the **Igreja do Carmo**, in the square of the same name on the east side of the river. Although plain on the outside, the inside is a Baroque extravaganza of gilt woodwork.

While you are on the east side of town, don't miss the lovely garden in Praça Dr António Padinha just over the old bridge, where sumptuous pink roses entwine a palm tree. In the square is a statue of a former bishop of the Algarve, Dom Marcelino Franco, who bears a rather uncanny resemblance to Steven Spielberg's ET.

Head to the riverfront for lively bars; the best **fish restaurants** are along the Rua José Pires Padinha.

> ### TAVIRA CHURCHES
>
> The interior of **São Sebastião** (Campo dos Mártires da Pátria) has paintings depicting the lives of Jesus and Mary. **Santo António** on the other side of the square, has a life-sized tableau of angels and saints at the funeral of St Anthony. The **São Francisco Monastery**, near the army barracks, has a wonderfully ornate façade.

The barrier islands of the eastern Algarve are important nurseries for fish such as bass, gillhead and bream, which lay their eggs in the sheltered waters. Only low-level local fishing is allowed within the National Park's boundaries. **Clam picking** has long been a way of life for the scattered fishing communities who live on the offshore islands; now shellfish farms augment the harvest. Fish farms where bass, bream and sole are reared are on the increase, many using former salt pans.

Opposite: *The design of this hayloft near Estorninhos has remained unchanged for thousands of years.*
Below: *Off to put octopus pots in a likely location.*

AROUND TAVIRA

On your way from Olhão to Tavira, do stop in **Luz de Tavira** and admire the fine Manueline style of the ornate side door of the parish church; the front doorway, by contrast, is an example of Renaissance style. You could also take a quick detour south to **Santa Luzia**, on the edge of the lagoon sheltered by **Ilha de Tavira**. The earthenware pots you see on the boats and quayside are not lobster pots as might be thought initially but octopus traps. There is nothing an octopus likes more than to clamber into a nice secure hidey hole, and Santa Luzia is the octopus capital of the Algarve.

The adventurous may like to try some tentacle slices with a drink. These are charcoal grilled after being air dried on wooden racks – quite delicious but not to everyone's taste. Take a stroll through the cobbled back streets and admire the fishermen's cottages which are tiled from top to bottom – a riot of geometric and floral patterns in a rainbow of colours.

On the coast east of Tavira, **Cabanas** and **Manta Rota** are two small but growing package holiday resorts. Both are quiet places with rather a lack of atmosphere, but are popular with families in July and August because of their good sandy beaches.

In this part of the Algarve tourist development is restricted to the coast, and driving just a couple of miles inland takes you into semi-wild countryside and the rolling hills of the **Serra de Alcaria do Cume**. Drive the 30km (20 miles) up to **Cachopo** and walk or drive with care along some of the unmade roads, and you will discover tiny remote farms where all cultiva-

tion is done by hand. Apart from a few new implements, things haven't changed much in thousands of years.

A much shorter circular drive of 25km (15 miles) which will give you a taste of the hill country, starts when you take the Fonte Salgada turn off from the EN125 which skirts Tavira. Follow the signs to Estorninhos and then turn right to return to the coast.

Here in the hills, rock roses and sweet-scented lavender run rampant, interspersed with tiny pockets of cultivation. Hay is generally still gathered by hand on the steep slopes and secured in little stooks, each tied with a single strand.

The curious round buildings with conical thatched roofs are haylofts, often with a tiled threshing floor just outside. These are a direct throwback to the Bronze Age. At that time circular buildings were easier to construct, and straight lines only became prevalent with the Romans. Some archaeologists believe that early civilizations preferred conical roofs because they mirrored the vault of the sky, and also the yurt-like tents used by nomadic tribes. Interestingly, many of the modern houses in the area also feature conical roofs. Old habits die hard in these parts.

Above: The Praça do Pombal in the centre of Vila Real de Santo António.

ON THE SPANISH BORDER

Vila Real de Santo António ★

Submerged by the sea in the 17th century and rebuilt by the Marquês de Pombal along a grid system in 1774, Vila Real de Santo António is architecturally like nowhere else in the Algarve. It is similar in design to the Baixa district in Lisbon, which Pombal also masterminded after the Great Earthquake.

The central square, the **Praça do Pombal**, features a striking black and white mosaic pavement, and is surrounded by lemon trees and elegant 18th-century town houses. Glance downwards to admire the fish motifs on the ornate wrought iron drains. All the building materials were brought from the capital – ironically, stone quarries were discovered in the vicinity a short while later.

The Guadiana River marks the boundary with Spain, and you can take a trip across the river on one of the frequent ferries to visit Ayamonte – which is rather a dull town. Don't forget your passport. Of perhaps more interest, **Seville** is only 170km (105 miles) away over the new road bridge, or you can take a day cruise upriver and enjoy the lovely scenery.

Souvenir shops cater for Spanish day trippers, while **Monte Gordo** on the coast sees plenty of Spanish holiday-makers in the summer. The big attraction has to be low Portuguese prices (accommodation and meals cost around a third less than average prices in Spain) because Monte Gordo is not one of the prettier resorts in the Algarve with its unattractive high-rise apartments. The beach is large, however, and there's a beachside casino for high rollers.

Castro Marim

Just 3km (2 miles) north of Vila Real de Santo António is Castro Marim, dominated by a huge hilltop **castle** built by King Afonso III in the 13th century. Destroyed by the 1755 earthquake, only the castle's outer walls remain, as do fragments of one of the churches within the walls.

Also within the walls are the remains of a smaller castle, the headquarters of the Order of Christ. It was built to a square plan with a circular tower at each of its corners. The fort of **São Sebastião** you can see from the walls was built in 1641, when the new royal dynasty, the Braganças, once again felt the need to fortify the border with Spain.

Beyond the fort the salt flats stretch around the Guadiana estuary. This is now a nature reserve: the **Reserva do Sapal**. Within the castle walls is an office where you can pick up a map of the reserve. Look out for flamingoes, storks, black-winged stilts and smaller birds such as sandpipers and plovers.

Above: *The fish motif appears on ornate drains in Vila Real de Santo António.*
Below: *Castro Marim.*

KNIGHTS TEMPLAR

The Templars were a religious order of knights, formed in Jerusalem in the 12th century to fight infidels and protect Christian pilgrims. Both the reigning powers and the Church became jealous of their plundered wealth and arrogance. Some said they practised the Black Arts, and many were well versed in Hermetic philosophy and classical occultism picked up in the Middle East. Many of the more lurid stories emerged under torture, so can probably be discounted. They were ex-communicated by the Pope in the 14th century, but immediately relaunched themselves in Portugal under a new name, the Order of Christ.

Alcoutim

The river drive from **Foz da Odeleite** up the Guadiana to Alcoutim is one of the loveliest in the Algarve. The land is lush, well watered and well wooded, with small plots of vines and corn along with olive groves. Pack a picnic, leave the car and go for a walk beneath sun-dappled branches, or take a leisurely boat trip upriver from Vila Real, with a barbecue lunch and swimming stops.

Alcoutim has been an important river port from Phoenician times onwards, although nowadays the river traffic is pleasure boats and yachts rather than merchant ships. From here you can take a cruise upriver to **Mértola** and get a flavour of the Alentejo, although the province's distinctive scenery starts a few miles further north. If you feel like a change from seafood, you could try some of the **river fish** which feature prominently on local menus. Eels, lamprey and carp are among the specialities.

The early 14th-century castle was where Fernando I signed a short-lived peace treaty with Henry of Castile. The castle of **Sanlucar de Guadiana**, on the Spanish side of the border, is a mute reminder of centuries of feuding.

The **mountain villages** to the west are where to find some of the most authentic handicrafts in the Algarve. Blankets, rugs, pottery and baskets are all made in the same way they were made centuries ago.

The road leading west to **Cachopo** takes you through some of the wildest scenery in the Algarve. But make sure you have enough petrol as filling stations are few and far between.

At Vaqueiros, near Martim Longo, visit an archeological reconstruction at **Parque Mineiros Cova Dos Mouros** that explores 5000 years of mining from Neolithic times onwards. There are donkey rides for children and hands-on activities.

Below: *A lace chimney pot, typical of those found in the region.*

Eastern Algarve at a Glance

BEST TIMES TO VISIT

Spring and autumn are ideal. Winters are mild, often sunny, but expect some rain between October and February. Summer can be hot but there is usually a breeze on the coast.

GETTING THERE

From Faro, **trains** or express **coach** services go to Tavira and Vila Real de Santo António. From Spain, cross the Guadiana by **ferry** from Ayamonte; if you have a **car** take the E01 motorway that crosses the river north of Castro Marim.

GETTING AROUND

Public transport is limited inland but a **bus** service connects the coastal resorts. Ask the local tourist office for details.

WHERE TO STAY

Olhão
Olhão has few recommended places, but the camp site on the **Ilha da Armona**, tel: 289 714 173, has beach chalets to rent.

BUDGET
Pensão Boemia, Rua da Cerca 20, tel: 289 714 513. Some rooms have balconies. Quiet and friendly.

Tavira
LUXURY
Convento de Santo António, Atalaia 56, tel: 281 325 632. Former monastery, now family-run hotel with 7 rooms. Antique furniture, lovely cloisters, quiet atmosphere.

MID-RANGE
Marés Residencial, Rua José Pires Padinha 134, tel: 281 325 815. Riverfront, popular with families; good food.
Quinta do Caracol, São Pedro, tel: 281 322 475, www.quinta docaracol.com Outside town, old converted farmhouse.
Vila Galé, tel: 281 329 900, www.vilagale.pt Stylish lowrise hotel on the outskirts of Tavira.
Quinta da Lua, Tavira, tel: 281 961 070. Outside town, guesthouse with pool and gardens, imaginative cookery including vegetarian options.

BUDGET
Pensão Residencial Lagôas, Rua Almirante Candido dos Reis 51, tel: 281 322 252. Roof terrace and courtyard.

Vila Real de Santo António
MID-RANGE
Hotel Guadiana, Avenida da República, tel: 281 511 482, fax: 281 511 478. Three-star hotel facing Guadiana River.

WHERE TO EAT

Olhão
Head to Avenida 5 de Outubro for fresh fish and seafood. Take your pick of a clutch of restaurants with sea views: **Papy's**, **Isidro**, **Cervejaria Ria**, **A Bote**, **Formosa** and **Livramento** are all worth trying.

Tavira
Restaurante O Patio, Rua Dr Antonio Cabrera 30, tel: 281

323 008. Roof terrace; *cataplanas* a speciality.
Marés Restaurante (*see* Where to Stay).
Restaurante Lagôas Bica, Rua Almirante Candido dos Reis 24, tel: 281 323 843. Inexpensive but very good.
Marisqueria 4 Aguas, Quatro Aguas, tel: 281 325 329. Just outside town on the east side, locally famous for its seafood.

Vila Real de Santo António
Caves do Guadiana, Avenida da República, tel: 281 544 498. Traditional cuisine, including *paella* for fans of this rice-based dish.

TOURS AND EXCURSIONS

Riosul, Rua Tristao Vaz Teixeira 15, Monte Gordo, tel: 281 510 200; Guadiana cruises, jeep safaris.
Turismar, Monte Gordo, tel: 281 956 634. Boat trips up the Guadiana, departing from Vila Real.
Centro Equestre Quinta do Cavalo, Monte Francisco, Castro Marim, tel: 281 531 385.

USEFUL CONTACTS

Tourist Offices
Olhão: Largo Sebastião, Martins Mestre, tel: 289 713 936; **Tavira:** Rua da Galeria, tel: 281 322 511; **Vila Real de Santo António:** Centro Cultural Antonio Aleixo, tel: 281 542 100. **Alcoutim:** Rua 1 de Maio, tel: 281 546 179. **Castro Marim:** Praça 1 de Maio, tel: 281 531 232.

6
The Alentejo

The Alentejo is Portugal's 'Big Country', a vast and sparsely populated rural province characterized by rolling grasslands, wheatfields and groves of oak and olive. It covers a third of Portugal but contains only a tenth of its population.

Baked by the sun to shades of ochre and gold in summer, and carpeted by wild flowers in spring, the countryside is a delight to nature lovers, photographers, and anyone interested in exploring one of the most distinctive but least known regions of western Europe.

Huge fields of golden ripening **wheat** ripple to the horizon, and in contrast to the mechanized cultivation recently introduced on the big estates, you will still see groups of gypsies camped by the roadside with their horses and mules.

For over 1500 years the Alentejo was subject to waves of invasions, and Romans, Visigoths, Moors, Spaniards and the French have come and gone, leaving behind a legacy of great fortified **castles**. **Évora** and **Vila Viçosa** have strong links with both of Portugal's royal dynasties of Avis and Bragança, while the former city was declared a UNESCO heritage site in 1986.

To visit the Alentejo is to take a step back in time – 50 years in terms of much of the agriculture, 400 for the sumptuous royal palaces from Portugal's Golden Age, 700 for the impressive medieval castles which crown the hills, and 4000 years when you discover the outstanding megalithic monuments.

DON'T MISS

★★★ **Beja:** the massive castle with an excellent view from the top of the keep.
★★★ **Convento da Nossa Senhora da Conceição:** the lavish convent at Beja.
★★★ **Évora:** the concentration of historic buildings.
★★★ **Estremoz and Vila Viçosa:** visit the marble towns.
★★★ **Prehistory:** a day in the countryside; discover dolmens and other prehistoric remains.
★★ **Wines:** the local wines should be sampled.

Opposite: *Spring flowers in the hills of the Serra d'Ossa.*

MÉRTOLA

Perhaps the most dramatic way to approach the Alentejo from the Algarve is to take the N122, which runs northwards from Vila Real de Santo António, parallel to the Guadiana River and the Spanish border.

When you cross the river Vascão you are in the Alentejo, but the landscape – barren upland moors – does not change significantly. Then suddenly you round a bend and there is Mértola, its imposing hilltop castle silhouetted against the sky.

At this point most visitors reach for their camera (there is a conveniently situated parking place on the right side of the road), but an even better panorama can be seen from the north, on the Serpa road just outside town.

Situated at the highest navigable point of the Guadiana, Mértola was visited by Phoenicians and Carthaginians sailing upriver to trade. The Romans called it Mirtilis, and shipped wheat, oil and wine (still staples of the local economy) south. There are traces of the original quay by the riverside.

Mértola is a good base for exploring the Guadiana valley, now a nature reserve. The lovely wooded countryside is rich in wildlife, including wild boar and birds of prey.

Castle ★★

The walls date from Moorish times but include some original Roman stonework; the keep was built in 1292 after the Christian reconquest. By both natural position and layout the castle must have been virtually impregnable.

Mesquita ★★

Next to the castle is the church, notable because it is one of only two former mosques to survive the Christian purge of Islam from Portugal. Inside are 12 Moorish columns supporting arabesque domes. The *mihrab*, or prayer niche, faces east to Mecca.

There are a few small museums dotted around town dedicated to Sacred Art, Islamic Art and Roman finds. For the best view of Mértola's large resident stork population, walk down Rua Combatantes de la Grand Guerra, and look along the river towards the **Convento de São Francisco**. These magnificent birds have built their nests on every available high wall and roof.

From Mértola you have a choice of routes north. The N122 to **Beja** is the faster of the two and will reveal the typical landscape of the southern Alentejo – endless wheatfields interspersed with stands of cork oak and olive trees.

Opposite: *Mértola's splendid castle dominates the skyline.*

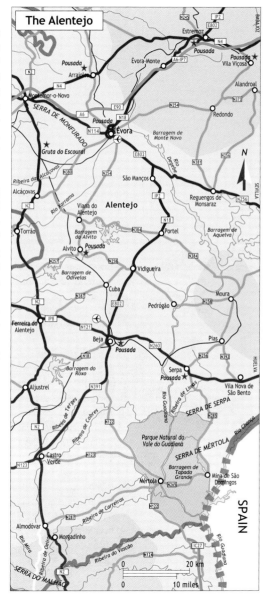

The Alentejo

Above: *The Capela de São Gens just outside Serpa was once a mosque.*
Opposite: *The cloisters of Beja's Convento da Nossa Senhora de Conceição.*
Below: *The entrance to Serpa Castle.*

SERPA

The Serpa road from Mértola winds upwards through hill country. The village of **Mina de São Domingo** is a collection of strikingly geometric white cottages with red-tiled roofs. Just outside the village one of the Guadiana's tributaries has been dammed to form a lake, and this is a good spot to pause for a refreshing swim in summer. There are steps down to the water, a diving board and a picnic area.

Serpa itself is a sleepy agricultural town. In the main square, the Praça da República, there's a good choice of cafés; glance upwards at the wrought iron lamp holders in the shape of dragons. If leaving the square by car take care to follow the signposted exits, otherwise you will find yourself in an impossibly narrow maze of lanes.

Castle ★★

Built by Dom Dinis after the Moors had been routed, the castle was badly damaged in 1707, when much of the town was blown up by the Spanish Duke of Ossuna during the Spanish **War of Succession**. Open daily 09:00–12:30 and 14:00–17:30.

You might take a peek in the rather grandly described 'museum' at the castle entrance; in fact it is just one room with a larger than life-sized tableau of the Last Supper. Also note the elegant aqueduct with an ingenious waterwheel mechanism.

Next to Serpa's *pousada* 2km (just over a mile) outside town, is the small **Capela de São Gens**, which was once a mosque. The only other surviving mosque is at Mértola.

BEJA

A busy, prosperous town and very hot in summer, Beja is the capital of the **Baixo** (lower) Alentejo, and by far the biggest town in the sparsely populated south. It's worth a visit if only for its magnificent **convent** and **castle**. Beja was a Roman provincial capital under the name of Pax Julia, and was where the peace treaty with the native Lusitanians was signed. After being conquered by the Moors in the 8th century AD it became a centre of Muslim scholarship. Beja sustained serious damage over centuries of wars with both the Spanish and the French, as well as during the Portuguese civil war; buildings of historical importance are limited.

The **Santa Amaro Church** just to the west of the castle is the oldest church in Beja, and parts of it date back to the Visigoths. The **Santa Maria**, situated in the square of the same name, is Gothic in style.

Nossa Senhora da Conceição Convent ★★★

Occupying the square of the same name, the convent dates from the 15th century and was formerly one of the richest and most important in the whole country. Architecturally it represents the transitional period from Gothic to Manueline forms. The 17th-century high altar in the church is an incredibly decadent affair, with bare-breasted sirens adding more than a touch of hothouse eroticism. Open 09:45–13:00 and 14:00–17:15; closed Mondays.

The Baroque processional of St John the Evangelist, which was carried through town on the saint's feast day, is over a metre (3.3ft) high. Surmounted by a gold filigree crown, it features a tableau of the saint about to be boiled in a cauldron, with two Moorish-looking figures lighting the fire.

THE PORTUGUESE NUN

Sister Mariana Alcoforado of the **Convento da Nossa Senhora da Conceição** had a secret love affair with a French officer who lived in Beja during the Spanish War of 1661–1668. The love letters she wrote to him after his departure were published in France as *Letters of a Portuguese Nun*. They scandalized Portuguese society but have since become classics of romantic literature. In 1972 they inspired three Portuguese women writers and poets to publish *The New Portuguese Letters*, which highlighted the plight of women under the Salazar dictatorship.

In the barrel vault of **John the Baptist's Court** are some wonderful blue and yellow *azulejo* tiles dating from the 17th century. By contrast, the **Chapter House** has Moorish tiles in a profusion of colours, abstract florals and geometric shapes.

The **museum** upstairs contains local artefacts from prehistoric times onwards, including some interesting runic inscriptions, Roman coins and mosaics.

The reconstruction of the terracotta grille through which the errant nun and her lover communed, provokes a certain amount of speculation by more lewd-minded visitors as to whether the relationship was consummated or not.

Castle ★★★

Another example of Dom Dinis's drive to defend the newly liberated kingdom against the emerging threat of Castile, the castle dates from 1303. Originally the outer wall had 40 towers; now only a few remain.

The view from the top of the 40m (130ft) keep (after mounting 190 steep steps) is impressive, taking in the handsome central courtyard with its ivy-covered walls, and the plains stretching out in all directions. Look downwards at the metal grilles strategically placed for pouring boiling oil on attackers – the last line of defence. Open Tuesday–Sunday 10:00–12:00 and 14:00–18:00.

Some 10km (6 miles) southwest of Beja, near the village of Penedo Gordo, are **Roman remains** dating from the 1st to 4th centuries AD. Among the structures uncovered are a villa, a bathhouses and some striking mosaics.

ÉVORA

Culturally, historically and politically important for centuries, Évora is a must-see on any itinerary. During the Middle Ages it was a centre of scholarship and the arts, attracting painters, architects, sculptors and writers. Its university dates from 1557.

It was one of the power centres of the royal Avis dynasty and Évora's citizens were instrumental in bringing the first king in the line, João I, to power in 1385. In recognition of this the royal court often met there. More darkly, it was also one of the main power bases of the Inquisition in Portugal. There are a wealth of sightseeing opportunities here.

Évora is a maze of cobbled streets, and it's easy to get lost with or without a map until you develop a sense of direction. Watch out for cars hurtling through back alleys. The traffic problem is becoming acute, and the city council is thinking of enforcing visitor parking just outside the city walls and laying on minibus transportation to the centre. Certainly you should park your car at the earliest possible opportunity.

Start exploring at the **Largo Marquês de Marialva**, which has the greatest concentration of monuments.

EARLY HISTORY

Évora received its name from the Celtic tribe referred to as **eburones** by the Romans. Ebora, as it was then called, was the capital of their kingdom. It was captured in the 2nd century BC by **Decimus Junius Brutus**, but it was not until 59BC that **Julius Caesar** completed the Romanization of the city. After the fall of Rome in the 5th century AD, the Visigoths took over, and lost Évora to the invading Moors in 711. Christian forces regained control in 1165.

Opposite: *Beja's splendid castle was said to be virtually impregnable.*
Below: *Old and even older, the Temple of Diana with the cathedral in the background.*

Temple of Diana ★★★

Built in the 2nd century AD, this is the best preserved Roman monument in Portugal, though marble plinths and six granite Corinthian columns are all that remain. It was partially destroyed during the persecutions of pagans by Christians in the 5th century AD, and was subsequently dismantled. It was then walled in and used as a slaughterhouse until 1870 before being restored.

Cathedral ★★

A large ostentatious building, and a good example of the transitional period between Romanesque and Gothic architecture, the cathedral dates from 1186, but the two towers were later additions, and the high altar and choirstalls were remodelled in Renaissance style in the 16th century. Open 09:00–12:00 and 14:00–17:00.

Within the building is the **Museum of Sacred Art**, where ornate gold chalices studded with gems, priestly regalia and portraits of bishops are on display. There is also an ivory statue of the Virgin which opens to reveal minutely detailed panels depicting the Annunciation, the Nativity and the Assumption.

Archbishop's Palace ★★★

Next door to the cathedral is the former palace of the powerful Archbishop of Évora, now housing the excellent **Regional Museum**. The building itself with its enormous vaulted roof is impressive, and on display are statues and fragments from Classical times onwards, many in the lovely cloisters. Also on the ground floor are some beautiful *azulejos*.

THE SOCIAL SCENE

Évora does not have a lively nightlife. The nearest it has to a social centre is the cavernous **Café Arcada** on the Praça do Giraldo. Much patronized by students and lecturers from the nearby university, it's a place in which to meet your friends, or to sit and read quietly over a **bica** or beer. You can have a snack, a full meal or one of the mouth-watering cakes. Try the local speciality *pasteis de Évora* – a tasty concoction made of eggs, butter, almonds, sugar and flour. The **Oficina Bar**, in Rua da Moeda, plays jazz and blues; **Praxis**, in Rua de Valdevinos, is the only really late club in town.

Opposite: *The inscription at the entrance to the bone chapel reads 'We bones that lie here wait for yours'.*

Convent dos Loios ★★

Also in the square is the Convent dos Loios, a 15th-century monastery now enjoying a new lease of life as a *pousada*. The adjoining **Church of São João Evangelista** has some fine *azulejos*, while next the **Paço dos Duques de Cadaval** (Palace of the Dukes of Cadaval) dates from the 14th century.

If the weight of history has left you gasping for refreshment, the solution is just on the doorstep. The Jardim do Paço serves drinks, meals and light snacks in a pleasant courtyard surrounded by orange trees. Outside in the square is a flower garden containing a plaque depicting Évora's coat of arms and some striking modern sculptures.

Church of Nossa Senhora da Graça ★★

The four giant figures dominating the façade of the church of Nossa Senhora da Graça (just south of the junction between the Rua Miguel Bombarda and Rua de República) have excited much speculation as to their significance. Some say that the giants, each holding a globe, celebrate Portugal's new-found domination of the four corners of the earth. A darker explanation suggests that, as the globes appear to be engulfed in flames they represent sub-human monsters burned by the Inquisition.

Church of São Francisco ★★★

Apart from the Largo Marquês de Marialva, this is Évora's most visited attraction. The main church dates from the 15th century (open 10:00–12:45 and 14:30–17:45), but the big attraction is the **Capela dos Ossos** or Bone Chapel.

The macabre bone chapel itself is packed with bones and skulls which once belonged to over 5000 monks. You enter the chapel through a side chapel, where an image of the suffering Christ is dressed in Portuguese workman's clothes. Take a look at the glass panel on the left – full of wax offerings in the shape of legs, arms and heads. These have been blessed in the hope that afflictions will be cured.

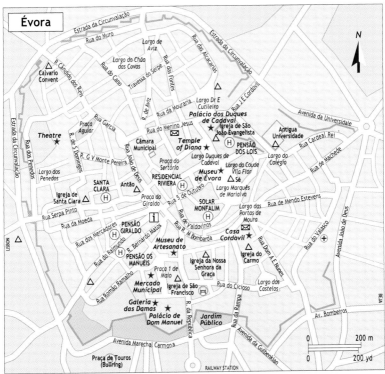

ALMENDRES STONE CIRCLE

Some visitors have noted a powerful forcefield emanating from the sandstone monolith with spirals and circles engraved on the face, just off centre. Try it yourself by standing about 2m (6ft) from the stone. The effect varies from nothing to definite spine tingling, depending on individual sensitivity, and perhaps on the fluctuating strength of the force itself. You may also care to experiment with walking between the gateways formed by pairs of stones.

Opposite: *Mysterious symbols on the standing stones of the Cromeleque dos Almendres.*
Below: *Entrance to the burial chamber of the Zambujeiro dolmen.*

DISCOVER ÉVORA'S PREHISTORIC PAST

The Alentejo has been inhabited for many thousands of years, although little is known about the human life and society in those distant times before recorded history. Megalithic construction of **dolmens**, **menhirs** and **stone circles** reached a high point in the third and fourth millennia BC.

While the area surrounding Évora has over 100 dolmens and other megalithic remains, many are in a poor state or are inaccessible. This route highlights three of the most interesting (a dolmen, menhir and stone circle), which are also easy to find. While some of the roads and tracks are on packed sand, this should not present any problems to cars except after heavy rain.

You will also have the bonus of discovering some of the prettiest countryside in the Alentejo, so allow plenty of time to enjoy the peace and birdsong. If you have the time, pack a picnic and make a day of it.

Take the N114 road from Évora to Lisbon and Montemor o Novo. After 10km (6 miles) take a left-hand turn signposted to **Guadalupe**. On reaching the village, turn left to Valverde and drive along the sand road. When you reach the junction with a surfaced road, turn

left. Take another left turn at the sign to Anta do Zambujeiro, and drive through the yard of the agricultural research station belonging to the University of Évora. Take the left-hand gate and park at the sign. Cross the stream and you'll see a huge dolmen, partially sheltered by a corrugated iron roof.

Anta do Zambujeiro ★★

Anta do Zambujeiro is the largest dolmen of its type in Europe, and the support stones of the chamber are 6m (20ft) in height and weigh several tons. The huge top stone has been removed to prevent further cracking, and lies on the west side of the mound. It was originally a burial chamber and later became a focus of cult worship; the granite is still being dated. Flint arrow heads, ceramic pots, amber beads and copper tools found here are on display in the **Museum of Évora**.

Now retrace your route back to Guadalupe and turn left at the junction, following the sign to the Cromeleque dos Almendres. When you reach **Monte dos Almendres** (a group of farm buildings; the site has been a farm since Roman times), park on the grass verge by the abandoned well, and head diagonally across the field towards the grain silos. Note the tiled threshing floor on your left. Here is the **Menhir dos Almendres** – a phallic stone approximately 4m (13ft) high with engravings near the top.

Now continue along the sand road, passing through a lovely cork oak wood. The landscape has a strange melancholic air and gives the impression of great antiquity. Stop by the picnic table and you will see the stone circle on your left.

Cromeleque dos Almendres ★★★

The Cromeleque dos Almendres consists of 95 stones, with smaller circles within the main circle. It is thought to date from around 2000BC and may have been used for astronomical calculations. Some of the stones have spiral and geometric patterns carved into their faces. Although its original purpose is unclear, the circle has been used for magical and religious ceremonies for millennia and it shows.

The whole place has a rather magical feel to it – not threatening but quite enchanting. Évora can be seen on the horizon and the woods are a lovely spot for a picnic.

ASKING THE WAY

Signposting is good in the Alentejo, but if you do lose your way you may have to ask a local, and many do not speak English. Even if you have memorized the question in Portuguese you may not understand the answer! So keep it simple, and ask questions which require a simple yes / no answer.
• Excuse me sir / madam
Faz o favor senhor / senhora
• To get to...?
Para ir a ...?
• Is it to the left / right / straight ahead?
é a esquerda / a direita / sempre en frente?
And don't forget to say *muito obrigado – obrigada* if you're female.

TRADITIONAL CLOTHES

When you're travelling in the countryside keep a look-out for **shepherds** wearing a *pelico* – a traditional dark brown sheepskin coat with a long tail. These are normally worn in the cold winter months and the shepherd sits on the tail. The **Capote Alentejano** is a caped coat, often with a fur trim – ideal for keeping out the elements. Farm workers and horsemen often wear leather chaps.

CASTLES, CHURCHES AND MORE DOLMENS: A CIRCULAR TOUR FROM ÉVORA

Viana do Alentejo ★★

This is the first stop after following the die-straight Roman road southwest from Évora. The 14th-century castle here looks like something out of a child's story book, with its sturdy ramparts linking four circular towers. Inside the castle walls is the extraordinary **Church of Nossa Senhora da Assunção**.

The walls are crenellated like the castle's, with fake canons pointing outwards and grotesque gargoyles as well. The doorway is a fine example of eclectic Manueline style – carved with swirls, flourishes, vines, flowers, guitar players, faces and dancers. The interior is Romanesque with Manueline embellishments.

Alvito ★

The powerful barons of Alvito built the **castle** here in 1494; unlike most other castles in Portugal it belonged to them rather than the crown. It's a rather robust example, with a circular turret at each corner and a square keep on the northern face. Now converted into a *pousada*, guests dine in the Great Hall where the barons once entertained royal guests.

Around the sleepy little town look out for examples of ornate Manueline stonework on arches, balconies and windowsills; the town well with two horseshoe arches is particularly striking. The **Igreja Matriz**, the parish church dating from the 15th century, is a handsome sandstone building with crenellated walls and a sundial.

Portel ★

Almost exactly equidistant between Évora and Beja, Portel was granted its royal charter in the 13th century. The handsome **castle**, flags fluttering in the breeze, dates from the same period. In more modern times the town's marching brass band has achieved local fame; you may be fortunate enough to catch them in action.

Other Dolmens ★

Returning to Évora along the IP2, turn left into the village of **São Manços** and head for the parish church. Cross the bridge and turn left at the signpost to **Torre de Coelheiros**. When you get to the strikingly fortified manor house on the outskirts of the village, turn right along a signposted track. After approximately 2km (1½ miles), park by a small reservoir and follow the stream to the first dolmen, where the chamber and 5m (16ft) passage are still intact.

The second dolmen (one of the largest in the area) is 300m (1000ft) to the southwest of the first across a wheatfield. There is usually a tractor track leading to the dolmen so you need not disturb the crop. The air is filled with the sound of the musical bells of sheep and cattle.

Returning to Torre de Coelheiros, turn left along a wider road which rejoins the main Évora road 7km (4½ miles) south of the city.

Above: *Alvito's castle is now a pousada, a luxury government hotel.*
Opposite: *The entrance to the church of Nossa Senhora da Assunção in Viana do Alentejo.*
Below: *The dolmens near Torre de Coelheiros.*

EARLY HISTORY

We know very little about the lifestyle of the people who built the Alentejo's impressive dolmens, but rather more about the **lusitani**. This Celtic/Iberian tribe resisted the Roman occupation around 200BC. They are said to have worn cloaks similar to the Capote Alentejano, preferred their hair long, liked elaborate jewellery and drank beer. It took the Romans the best part of 70 years to subdue them.

Above: *Évora-Monte, a mountain-top village with a 16th-century Manueline-style castle near Évora.*

ÉVORA-MONTE ★

Located halfway between Évora and Estremoz, the **castle** is an unmistakable sight from the road. Close up it is less impressive. Looking rather like a giant sandcastle, it is in fact a modern reconstruction, but built on the cheap from sand and cement render. Inside, the exhibits include old looms – the area is famous for its carpet weaving.

The view from the castle is glorious. This was where the **War of the Two Brothers** was concluded in 1834 by the signing of a peace treaty. The original castle was built by Dom Dinis in 1312. It was destroyed in an earthquake in 1531, and rebuilt a few years later with the chunky towers on which the current version is based.

ESTREMOZ ★★★

This is one of the most rewarding and atmospheric towns to visit in the Alentejo. Kings and queens have lived and died here, and Estremoz was the centre of several decisive military 7aigns against the Spanish during the wars of independence and succession.

The best place to begin your exploration is the **Rossio** – a huge square which holds a fascinating Saturday morning market. If you want to buy a live chicken, a seedling lemon tree, or some of the lupin seeds (*tremoços*) which gave the town its name, this is the place. Look out also for red Estremoz pottery.

The tourist office is on the south side of the square, next to the town hall. Take a look in the latter (enter by the Police Station door), and admire the blue *azulejos* depicting historical and biblical scenes, which run up the staircase. This fine 17th-century building was once a convent dedicated to St Philip of Nery, a local bishop, and his life is detailed in some of the *azulejos*.

The town's hospital on the east side of the square is also housed in a former convent. Next door is the **Museu Rural**, which provides an insight into rural life in the Alentejo over the last 50 years. Open 10:00–13:00 and 15:00–17:00.

Still in the Rossio, admire the crumbling but still elegant façade of the **Igreja de São Francisco** (the Gothic monastery next door is now a cavalry barracks), and cast a glance at **Lago do Gadhana**, the ornamental lake just opposite. The bearded 17th-century statue in the centre looks like Neptune, but the scythe rather suggests Saturn.

MIRACULOUS APRON

Dom Dinis's wife Isabel was deeply touched by the plight of the poor, and used to distribute food to needy families. She was later canonized for her good works. Dinis ordered her to cut back on her charity work but she continued in secret. One day the king caught her hurrying from the palace with a bundle wrapped in her apron. He asked her to show him what she was carrying, and she opened her apron to discover that the bread had miraculously turned into roses. This charming legend is depicted by the statue within the castle walls.

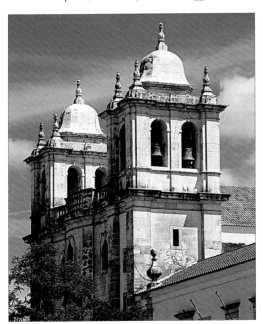

Left: *There are some fine* azulejos *inside Estremoz's town hall.*

THE FOOD OF ALENTEJO

Pork is the king of Alentejana cuisine. The local pigs are lean, dark and primitive; their diet consists largely of acorns. *Perna de porco* is leg marinated in red pepper paste and then roasted; *carne de porco Alentejano* is marinated pork stewed with clams; *migas* is fried pork with bread. Need a quick snack? Try a *bifana* – hot pork served in a crusty roll with mustard on the side. If you are an adventurous eater try *orelhas* (stewed ears) or *pezinhos* (trotters). *Borrego* (lamb) and *cabrito* (kid) are also excellent. *Sopa de tomate Alentejana* is a meal in a dish – as well as tomatoes it contains fresh coriander, green beans, onions, fried bread and a poached egg.

Just behind the lake is a small fountain, the **Fonte das Bicas**. This has nothing to do with coffee – *bica* also means a spout and this fountain has several.

If you could do with a drink, the most interesting café to head for is Café Alentejano on the Rossio square. It's full of old-timers discussing the price of feed. If you want to blend in you might consider purchasing a flat hat – to be worn at a jaunty angle. At the bar, pride of place is taken by a whole roast suckling pig destined to be carved into *bifanas* – hot pork rolls.

There's more rural flavour at the **Museu Alfaia Agricola** (Rua Serpa Pinto, open 09:00–12:30 and 14:00–17:30; closed Mondays). Browse through agricultural and household implements which illuminate the region's traditions. Many items similar to these exhibits are still in use on farms, having been handed down for generations.

On your way up to the castle look down at the elegant black and white pavements made out of local marble laid out in geometric designs. The Praça de Camões is a good example.

Castle ★★★

The walls survive, but all that remains of the 13th-century royal castle is the tower. Built of grey marble and 27m (90ft) high, it was known as the **Tower of the Three Crowns** because it was built by three kings: Sancho II, Afonso III and Dom Dinis.

After Dom Dinis's death the adjoining royal palace was used as an ammunition dump, which blew up in 1698. What is left of the palace has been converted into a luxurious *pousada*.

Through the grille of the tiny chapel of **Santa Isabel** *azulejos* depicting the life of the saintly queen, the wife of Dom Dinis, can be seen. The site was formerly her palace. The room where she died was later turned into a chapel, in thanks for the decisive Portuguese victory against the forces of Castile.

In the battle of the Lines of Elvas, 8000 foot soldiers and 2500 cavalry from Estremoz engaged a Spanish army four times larger and carried the day, leaving 10,000 of the enemy dead and losing just 800 men.

The **Municipal Museum** is located in the same square and contains clay figurines depicting peasant life and religious themes, along with old firearms and furniture. Upstairs is a reconstruction of a typical country kitchen. Open 10:00–12:30 and 14:00–17:00, closed Mondays.

Opposite left: *The name Lago de Gadhana means Scythe Lake.*
Opposite right: *The many-spouted Fonte das Bicas.*
Below: *Climb to the top of the castle keep for a fine view of Évora in the southwest and the Spanish sierras to the east.*

Above: *Statue of Dom João with the Paço Ducal in the background.*

VILA VIÇOSA ★★★

This is perhaps the most striking of the **marble** towns. Old town houses have wrought iron balconies, ornate door knockers and marble windowsills and doorways. Rua Dr Couto Jardim, which runs from Praça da República to the **Ducal Palace**, has many of the best examples.

Lined with orange trees and paved with marble, the **Praça de República** is a pleasant square, and where you will find both the tourist office and the castle. Also in the square is the **Igreja de São Bartolomeu**, formerly a 17th-century Jesuit college. It still has a town house façade but a Gothic/Renaissance interior.

Castle ★★

Built by the ubiquitous Dom Dinis in the 13th century, the castle was rebuilt in the 16th century in the Italian style which was then in vogue. It has seen plenty of action over the centuries, having defended Vila Viçosa against various Spanish armies and also Napoleonic forces during the Peninsula War.

Within the castle is a **Museum of Hunting** containing several rooms of sad-looking trophies, ranging from big game to tiny birds. The collection of hunting rifles is impressive, however, and there is also an interesting display of African weapons, including a spear with a shotgun-shaped stock, presumably carved to endow it with similar power and accuracy. The museum is open 09:30–13:00 and 14:00–18:00.

Within the castle walls (from which there are fine views of both the town and the surrounding countryside) are a cemetery and the 16th-century **Church of Nossa Senhora da Conceição**.

Paço Ducal ★★★

This monolithic palace, in grey and ochre marble, dominates a great square containing an equestrian statue of **Dom João IV**, 8th Duke of Bragança, and the first of that dynasty to succeed to the throne.

The **Braganças** had long been the most powerful family in Portugal, and monarchs of the House of Avis had often attempted to clip their wings. After the House of Avis came to an heirless end in 1580, Philip II of Spain stepped into the vacuum, but in 1640 the Spanish governor of Portugal was deposed in Lisbon and, by popular acclaim, João was crowned King of Portugal.

Left: *Vila Viçosa's castle is entered in the traditional way via a drawbridge.*

The palace as we see it today was built in 1573, but the first Bragança residence on the site dated from 1502. Even after the Braganças moved to Lisbon and had their pick of sumptuous palaces, they retained an affection for Vila Viçosa and their adjoining hunting estate, now a game reserve, and spent many summers here.

The palace is now a museum, and tour guides will show you around the sumptuous collections of tapestries, porcelain, paintings, frescoes and oriental carpets. These were bequeathed to the nation by the last King of Portugal, Dom Manuel II, who died in exile in London in 1932. His father, Carlos I, was a keen amateur painter and spent his last night here before his assassination in Lisbon in 1908.

You can look out over formal gardens designed in the Versailles style, and also visit the vast kitchens, which have what is claimed to be the largest collection of copper pots in Europe – all 709 of them. There is also a carriage collection, and an armoury featuring weaponry from medieval times up to the turn of the century. To the left of the palace is the 16th-century **Convento das Chagas**, which has been transformed into a *pousada*.

MARBLE FROM VILA VIÇOSA AND ESTREMOZ

Travelling between Estremoz and Vila Viçosa, you can't fail to spot the huge marble quarries just outside the town of **Borba**. The marble produced here is among the best in the world and much of it is exported to Italy. As well as being used for buildings locally, marble chips can be heated in an earth oven (*forno de cal*) to produce whitewash after water has been added. Local houses are whitewashed every year as *cal* is cheap but not very durable. Oxides are added to produce the characteristic blue and ochre shades.

DAMMED SPOT

The Barragem de Alqueva to the west of Reguengos de Monsaraz, where the Guadiana has been dammed, is the biggest artificial lake in Europe, 85km (52 miles) long with a 1200km (746-mile) shoreline. It was built to alleviate the Alentejo's chronic water shortages. The villages of Alqueva, Amiera and Estrela on the new lake shore now offer sailing, fishing and canoeing trips. However, Friends of the Earth has condemned the scheme as 'the biggest ecological crime ever committed in Portugal', claiming that the damage done to the environment and wildlife of the Guadiana valley outweighs any benefits.

SOUTH TO MONSARAZ

If you feel like a change of scenery from the Alentejo landscape, go for a drive through the **Serra d'Ossa**. This range of hills is not very high – the highest point is 653m (2155ft), but is very pretty and wooded with eucalyptus, pine and oak.

Take the road south from Estremoz to Redondo, which will pass through the small village of **Aldeia da Serra**. Just before you reach the village on the left is the 16th-century **Convento de São Paulo**, now tastefully converted into a luxury hotel. The original *azulejos* and frescoes remain. Above the village is the little church of **Monte Virgem**, built on the site of an earlier hermitage and with lovely views over the hills.

The nearby town of **Redondo** has the almost obligatory castle which was granted a royal charter by Afonso III in 1270. But it's the name of the castle gate, **Porta da Ravessa**, that everyone remembers. This is the name of an excellent wine which comes in red and white; the full-bodied red has won prizes. It is produced by the local winery: the **Adega Cooperativa de Redondo**. The town is also notable for traditional potteries.

Reguengos de Monsaraz also produces some rather excellent wines; the name Reguengos refers to the grassland outside town once owned by the Braganças. It is famous for its festivals, and the main ones are held in January, May and August, but there are plenty of interim saint's day festivities. Reguengos is a modern town for these parts, and has developed as an agricultural satellite of the far older Monsaraz just down the road. Sheep and grain farming were once important, but **wine production** (there is a town co-operative) has now taken over as the mainstay of the local economy.

Monsaraz ★★★

This little village, perched on a steep hill and visible for miles around, is one of the most atmospheric places in the Alentejo. Cobbled lanes, low-rise old houses and of course the castle, make you feel you've stepped back in time to medieval days.

Strategically placed overlooking the Guadiana River, Monsaraz has been inhabited since prehistoric times, and Romans, Visigoths and Moors all took advantage of the hill's defensive potential. Dom Dinis added the castle and fortified walls in the 14th century, and from the ramparts you can gaze west across the plains (the coast is just visible on clear days), or east to the Spanish *mesas* across the Guadiana. In the open square outside the castle, bullfights are held on saint's days during summer.

The tourist office is in the main square, as is the **Igreja Matriz de Santa Maria do Castelo** (parish church) which contains an ornate marble tomb dating from the 13th century. Next door is a small religious museum containing a 14th-century fresco of a judge being simultaneously tempted by the devil and encouraged by the majestic justice of Christ.

Outside Monsaraz

The little village of **São Pedro do Corval**, on the Reguengos road, is a good place to buy plates, pots and other locally produced ceramics.

There are a number of interesting prehistoric monuments at the foot of the hill. Look out for the **Menhir de Bulhoa** on the left side of the dirt road from Telheiro to Outeiro. The **Dolmen of Olival da Pega** is signposted to the right just after you leave the village on the Reguengos road; the **Xarez** stone circle is off the road to Mourão. Take the right-hand track just before the sign to Quinta de Jerez.

Above: *Horta de Moura, a small luxury hotel just outside Monsaraz.*
Opposite: *The old part of Redondo lies just through the gates.*

SHOPPING

Ceramic dishes painted in bright colours with floral or geometric patterns are good buys everywhere. **Redondo** is particularly famous for its potteries; blue and yellow are traditional colours. Alentejan specialities include idealised paintings of country life and small figurines from **Estremoz**. Locally made leather and sheepskin jackets and waist-coats can be bought in the markets. In **Mértola** and **Reguengos de Monsaraz** you can buy handwoven rugs and blankets in natural colours. Évora has some good handi-craft shops in and around the Praça Giraldo. Fine Alentejano wines make a good souvenir, and names to look out for include Reguengos VQRPD and Porta da Ravessa.

The Alentejo at a Glance

Spring (March–May) and autumn (late September to November) are the best times for a touring or active holiday; temperatures are pleasant and the risk of rain less than in the winter. Summers can be very hot and you may find a pool an asset. Winter nights can be chilly but you should get your fair share of fine sunny days; pack some layers and rainwear just in case.

The transport hubs of the Alentejo are Évora for the north and Beja for the south. There are several daily **express bus services** from Lisbon to Évora taking around two hours; the less frequent **railway service** takes at least three. Beja is served by **express coaches** from both Lisbon and Faro, via Albufeira. If coming by **car**, new motorways have cut the time it takes to reach Évora from Lisbon to under two hours. If you're coming from the Algarve, the quickest route is to take the fast IP1 dual carriageway from just north of Albufeira. Should you have a bit more time on your hands, the road from São Bras de Alportel to Almodovar winds over the hills of the Serra do Caldeirão; if you're driving from the eastern Algarve the road from Vila Real de Santo António to Mértola runs parallel to the Guadiana river.

A car is recommended as public transport (effectively buses – trains are dispiritingly slow) is not that frequent. Having said that, from Beja you'll be able to connect with Serpa, Évora and Mértola. Estremoz and Vila Viçosa are served by buses from Évora. Change at Reguengos for buses to Monsaraz.

Évora
LUXURY
Pousada Dos Lois, Largo Marques de Marialva, tel: 266 730 070, www.pousadas.pt Restored convent in centre of town opposite Roman temple.

MID-RANGE
Solar Monfalim, Largo da Misericórdia, tel: 266 750 000, www.monfalimtur.pt Comfortable central property, formerly an aristocrat's house.

BUDGET
Pensão Giraldo, Rua dos Mercadores 27, tel: 266 705 833.

Several quintas (country manors) in the countryside around town offer B&B; the tourist office can supply details and help with bookings.

Alvito
LUXURY
Pousada Castelo de Alvito, tel: 284 480 700, fax: 284 485 383. Within the 15th-century castle, with outdoor pool.

Estremoz
LUXURY
Pousada Rainha Santa Isabel, Largo de Dom Dinis, tel: 268 332 075, www.pousadas.pt Converted castle overlooking town, with antiques and modern comforts such as a pool.

MID-RANGE
Hospedaria Dom Dinis, Rua 31 de Janeiro 46, tel: 268 332 717. Good value for money, modern part of town.

BUDGET
Pensão Mateus, Rua de Almeida 39, tel: 268 322 226. Central location, friendly.

Vila Viçosa
LUXURY
Pousada de Dom João IV, tel: 268 980 742, www.pousadas.pt Newly restored former convent attached to the duke's palace.

MID-RANGE
Casa de Peixinhos, tel: 268 980 472, fax: 268 881 348. On Borba road, 17th-century manor house just outside town; marble and antiques.

Aldeia da Serra (near Redondo)
LUXURY
Hotel Convento de São Paulo, tel: 266 989 160, www.hotel conventospaulo.com Former convent; gardens, pool, views.

Monsaraz
MID-RANGE
Horta da Moura, tel: 266 550 100, www.hortadamoura.pt

The Alentejo at a Glance

In lovely valley outside town, with pool, horses and bikes for hire.

Beja
LUXURY
Pousada de São Francisco, tel: 284 313 580, www. pousadas.pt Beautifully converted Franciscan monastery with original stonework, Gothic arches, marble floors and pool.

Serpa
LUXURY
Estalagem São Gens, tel: 284 540 420. Located just outside town; modern four-star hotel with pool.

WHERE TO EAT

All the *pousadas* listed above have fine (if expensive) restaurants featuring regional dishes.

Évora
Restaurante Cozinha de Santo Humberto, Rua da Moeda 39, tel: 266 704 251, fax: 266 742 367. Regional specialities, popular with locals.
Café Arcada, Praça do Giraldo 10. Popular with university students and lecturers, this huge buzzy bar/café serves drinks, snacks and light meals.

Estremoz
Adega dos Isaias, Rua do Almeida 21, tel: 268 322 318. Authentic local dishes in suitably rustic atmosphere.
Café Alentejano, Rossio 16, tel: 268 337 300. Good filling local food in the upstairs restaurant.

Beja
Adega Tipica 25 Abril, Rua da Moeda. A rustic surrounding, has good food and very reasonable prices.
Entrearcos, Rua Jorge Raposo 13. Lovely ambience. Try the 'petiscos' – the Alentejo version of tapas.

Monsaraz
Café Restaurante O Alcaide, Rua de Santiago 18, tel: 266 557 158. Probably one of the best authentic restaurants in town, with lovely views too. Fantastic food.

Mértola
Restaurante Alengarve, Avenida Aureliano, tel: 286 612 210. Established traditional restaurant and a good place to try the local speciality – *javali* (wild boar).

TOURS AND EXCURSIONS

Bike Lab, Évora tel: 266 735 500, Beja tel: 284 325 313. Bicycle hire.
Turaventur, www.turaventur. com Évora, tel and fax: 266 743 134; biking, hiking, canoeing and jeep tours of the area for small groups (minimum of six people).

Mendes & Murteira, Rua 31 de Janeiro 15a, Évora, tel: 266 739 240, www.evora-mm.pt Offers tours of the city and megalithic sites; riding and jeep safaris.
Tiago Kalisvaart Riding School, Reguengos de Monsaraz, tel: 962 653 711. Explore the beautiful countryside on horseback. Beginners can take lessons.

USEFUL CONTACTS

Tourist Offices
Évora: Praça do Giraldo, tel: 266 777 071.
Estremoz: Largo da Republica, tel: 268 333 541.
Portel: Camara Municipal, Largo D. Nuno Alvares Pereira, tel: 266 619 030.
Monsaraz: Largo D. Nuno Alvares Pereira, tel: 266 557 136.
Viana do Alentejo: Praça da Republica, tel: 266 953 106.
Vila Viçosa: Camara Municipal, tel: 268 881 101.
Beja: Rua Capitão João Francisco de Sousa, tel: 284 311 913.
Mértola: Rua de Igreja 31, tel: 286 610 109.
Serpa: Largo D. Jorge 2/3, tel: 284 544 727.

ÉVORA	J	F	M	A	M	J	J	A	S	O	N	D
AVERAGE TEMP. °C	9	10	12	14	16	20	24	25	20	18	12	10
AVERAGE TEMP. °F	48	50	54	58	61	68	75	77	68	65	54	50
RAINFALL mm	81	71	96	56	46	8	5	3	38	58	76	79
RAINFALL in	3.2	2.8	3.8	2.2	1.8	0.3	0.2	0.1	1.5	2.3	3	3.1
DAYS OF RAINFALL	12	9	13	7	6	3	2	–	5	7	10	10

Travel Tips

Tourist Information

The Portuguese National **Tourist Office** is now part of an umbrella promotional organization called ICEP – short for Investimentos, Comércio e Turismo de Portugal.

Main Overseas Offices:
UK: 11 Belgrave Square, London SW1X 8PP, tel: (0845) 355 1212; **Ireland:** 54 Dawson Street, Dublin 2, tel: 1800 943 131, fax: (01) 670 9141; **South Africa:** 5th Floor, Mercantile Lisbon House, 142 West Street, Johannesburg 2193, tel: (011) 302 0404; **Canada:** 60 Bloor Street West, Suite 1005, Toronto M4W 3B8, tel: 1800 PORTUGAL; **USA:** 590 Fifth Avenue, 4th floor, New York 10036, tel: 1800 PORTUGAL, fax: (212) 764 6137; 88 Kearny Street, Suite 1770, San Francisco 94108, tel: 1800 PORTUGAL, fax: (415) 391 7147; **Australia:** 234 George Street, Sydney, tel: 292 412 710.
In **Lisbon** ICEP's HQ is: Palacio Foz, Praça dos Restauradores, 1200 Lisbon, tel: 21 346 3311; fax: 21 352 5810. **Algarve Tourist Board:** Avenida 5 de Outubro 18, 8000 Faro, tel: 289 800 400, helpline: 808 781 212.

Entry Requirements

Visitors from European Union countries, Australia, New Zealand, the USA and Canada only need a **valid passport** to enter Portugal. South Africans require a **visa**; visitors of other nationalities are advised to check current requirements before travel. For stays of more than 90 days a residency permit is required. EU visitors can arrange this locally, but other nationalities may have to leave Portugal and then re-enter the country.

Embassies:
Australia, tel: 213 101 500; Canada, tel: 213 164 651; New Zealand, tel: 213 509 690; South Africa, tel: 213 535 713; UK, tel: 282 490 750; Ireland, tel: 213 929 440; USA, tel: 217 273 300.

Customs

The duty-free allowance for travellers aged over 17 arriving from a non EU country is: 200 cigarettes or 100 cigarillos or 50 cigars or 250g of rolling tobacco; 1 litre of spirits or 2 litres of wine; 250cc of perfume. If arriving from the EU you can bring in any amount of duty-paid goods provided you can prove they are for your personal use, not for resale. Current guidelines suggest 800 cigarettes, 10 litres of spirits and 90 litres of wine but as prices for these goods are low in Portugal it is hardly worth the bother; you may instead consider buying them in Portugal if you're departing to another EU nation. There are no currency controls but you are obliged to tell customs if you are importing or exporting large amounts of money.

Health Requirements

Yellow fever certificate required if arriving from an infected area. Travellers are recommended to take out travel insurance policies which cover emergency medical care.

Getting There

By Air: TAP Air Portugal (www.tap.pt) serves Lisbon from most major European cities, plus New York, Johannesburg and other African and South American countries. Direct charter flights to Faro are widely available in the UK, Germany, Holland and Sweden. The best fares can usually be found in the UK, where 'no frills' airlines such as EasyJet and Monarch have helped to bring prices down.

By Road: From northern Spain the quickest route into Portugal is via Salamanca, crossing the Portuguese border at Vilar Formoso. From Madrid, the southwestern route to Badajoz on the border will bring you right into the Alentejo. Coming from Seville, Vila Real de Santo António on the Algarve coast is just 153km (97 miles) away. There are express coach services between Lisbon and Faro; these can be booked through local travel agencies.

By Rail: Portugal is a long train journey away from any European country except Spain. The two main routes run from Paris through northern Spain and Portugal to Lisbon, and from Madrid to Lisbon. There are regular services from Lisbon to Tunes in the Algarve, from where you can change to local services heading either east or west.

On the net: www.visit portugal.com – covers all of Portugal; www.visitalgarve.pt and www.visitalentejo.pt – tourist information; www.pousadas.pt – stay at historic castles, monasteries and manor houses; www. solaresdeportugal.pt – small inns, historic houses and small-scale rural accommodation; www.orbitur.pt and www.roteiro-campista.pt – camp sites.

What to Pack

From June to September pack lightweight summer clothes. In April/May and October/

USEFUL PHRASES

Hello • *Olá*	Viewpoint • *Miradouro*
Good Morning • *Bom dia*	Swimming Pool • *Piscina*
Good Afternoon • *Boa tarde*	Market • *Mercado*
Good Night • *Boa noite*	Petrol Station •
Please • *Por favor*	*Bomba de gasolina*
Thank you •	Police Station • *Polícia*
Obrigado (if male)	
Obrigada (if female)	**Numbers:**
Yes/No • *Sim/Não*	One •
How much is...? • *Quanto...?*	*Um* (if male)
Where is...? • *Onde é...?*	*uma* (if female)
Airport • *Aeroporto*	Two •
Railway Station •	*Dois* (if male)
Estação de comboios	*duas* (if female)
Bus Station •	Three • *Três*
Estação de camionetas	Four • *Quatro*
Bus Stop • *Paragem*	Five • *Cinco*
Church • *Igreja*	Six • *Seis*
Cathedral • *Sé*	Seven • *Sete*
Museum • *Museu*	Eight • *Oito*
Beach • *Praia*	Nine • *Nove*
Castle • *Castelo*	Ten • *Dez*

November, add a warm jacket and a few layers to cope with any unseasonably cool weather. In winter and early spring you will need a mixture of cottons and warmer clothes. A lightweight rainproof jacket is useful outside the summer months. Suits or jacket and tie (for men) and smart clothes (for women) are worn for business. Bathing suits should not be worn around town, but shorts are common attire for both men and women in resort areas in summer. Women will however attract less attention in remote rural areas or the Alentejo by wearing a skirt or trousers.

Money Matters

Currency: Like most of Western Europe, Portugal has adopted the euro, so you don't need to change money if you are arriving from Spain. Exchange rates do fluctuate, but a euro is roughly equivalent in value to the US dollar. The euro notes in circulation are in 5, 10, 20, 50, 100, 200 and 500 euro denominations, and there are 1 and 2 euro coins, as well as cents (100 cents to the euro) with values ranging from 1 to 50.

Exchange: Normal banking hours are from 08:30–15:00 Monday to Friday. The desk marked *câmbios* is the place where you can change traveller's cheques; don't forget your passport. Traveller's cheques may also be exchanged at the reception desk of many hotels and apartments. An increasing number of banks have automatic teller machines where you can withdraw currency 24 hours a day using a debit or credit card. Major credit cards are widely accepted in shops, restaurants and garages, but in rural areas it is wise to carry cash.

Tipping: Restaurant and hotel bills include a service charge, but a tip of 5–10% is normal for good service; the same applies to taxi drivers. Hotel porters will also appreciate a small tip.

Accommodation

The Algarve has a vast number of apartments and villas to rent as well as hotels.

Hotels are divided into the familiar categories of one to five stars. **Pensions** (*pensão*) and the very similar *residencials* are cheaper and are graded from one to three stars. These are often clean, comfortable and well run; private facilities are standard except in rural areas. Rooms are also available to rent in private houses. Look for the sign *quartos* or *dormidas*. There are 23 **camp sites** in the Algarve which range from one to four stars. At the top end you can expect restaurants, a pool and sports facilities, at the lower end not much beyond a shower block. *Ad hoc* camping on the beach is prohibited. There is a wide choice of places to stay which offer real Portuguese flavour.

Estalagems are inns roughly equivalent to a small four-star hotel, while the *Turismo de Habitação* scheme provides grants for owners of mansions or houses of historic or architectural interest to provide facilities for guests. *Turismo Rural* is a similar scheme applying in rural areas.

Pousadas are government-run hotels located either in historic buildings such as castles and convents, or more modern properties in areas of great natural beauty. Exclusive and expensive, they are run to high international standards but retain a great deal of Portuguese character. There are 62 *pousadas* in Portugal.

Tourist Offices, both local and overseas, can provide information on all types of accommodation available but cannot (officially at least) recommend or make bookings on your behalf.

Eating Out

There is an enormous choice of restaurants and cafés in the Algarve, less so in the Alentejo. There is a high turnover of managers and chefs in the Algarve so standards can fluctuate. Menus are posted outside so you can get an idea of prices before committing yourself. Portions are large. Shellfish is almost invariably the most expensive dish on the menu and is often marked PV, short for *preço variável*. In this case the price per kilo is quoted at current market rates. All restaurants are required to offer a set *menu de turista* which is often good value, as is the

prato do dia or dish of the day. House wines are generally good and represent excellent value for money.

Transport

Car Hire: A valid domestic or international driving licence is required to rent a car, and you must be over 23. Car hire is inexpensive by European standards. All the leading international companies have a desk at Faro airport. Often more competitive rates can be obtained by pre-booking a car abroad rather than on arrival. Holiday Autos (www.holidayautos.com) is a useful broker. Auto Jardim (tel: 800 200 613, www.auto-jardim.com) is a reliable local firm.

Road Rules: Driving is on the right and speed limits are 50kph (30 mph) in town, 90kph (55 mph) outside built up areas, 100kph (62 mph) on national roads (look for the N or EN prefix) and 120kph (75 mph) on motorways. If driving in a remote rural area it's advisable to keep the petrol tank topped up, particularly on Sundays and public holidays. Most hire cars take either super or unleaded (*sem chumbo*) petrol. The standard of driving in Portugal is appalling and the fatality rate is among the highest in Europe: 35 per 100,000 population compared to seven per 100,000 in the UK. Hire the best car you can afford. Grade C is the minimum you should consider but go higher if you can. A larger engine size will give you the extra acceleration you need to overtake or get out of trouble.

ROAD SIGNS

Abrande • Slow down
Atenção • Attention
Cuidado • Caution
Curva perigosa •
Dangerous bend
Dê prioridade • Give way
Desvio • Diversion
Espere • Wait
Estacionamento proibido •
No parking
Obras na estrada •
Road works
Parque de estacionamento •
Car park
Passagem proibida • No entry
Perigo • Danger

Mild-mannered and relaxed most of the time, the Portuguese turn into demons behind the wheel. Overtaking on blind corners and hills is commonplace, as is overtaking three abreast. If you intend overtaking, always check over your left shoulder to makesure the car behind you is not about to overtake you. Indicating, whether on roundabouts, intersections or when over-taking, is not common.
The EN125 which runs the length of the Algarve, is a dangerous road, and you should be prepared for any-thing, including being forced off the road and on to the hard shoulder. In rural areas drive carefully and be prepared for herds of animals, donkey carts or tractors on the road.
Drink driving laws exist but are not always adhered to. You may however be stopped and breathalyzed and if you fail there are stiff penalties.

When driving keep your pass-port with you at all times, otherwise you risk an on-the-spot fine from the local police. The Automovel Club de Por-tugal, tel: 289 898 950 (707 509 510 in an emergency), has reciprocal arrangements with a number of overseas motoring organizations, and publishes a good road map of Portugal; www.acp.pt
Buses: Local buses connect the main resorts; ask at the tourist office for details. Details of long-distance buses can be found on www.rede-expressos.pt and www.eva-bus.com
Trains: The regional railway line runs from Vila Real de Santo António in the east to Lagos in the west, with several trains daily in each direction. Most stop at all 47 stations in between, so get an express train if you are going far. Some stations (e.g. Albufeira and Silves) are located outside the town itself, but those at Vila Real de Santo António, Tavira, Faro, Portimão and Lagos are more convenient. Timetable details can be obtained from the tourist offices or Faro station; www.cp.pt
Taxis: There are taxi ranks in all the major towns, also radio taxis. Fares from Faro airport to resorts are set, so establish the price first. Otherwise you pay what is on the meter or, if it's a long way, by agreeing a price with the driver.

Business Hours

Office hours usually 09:00–13:00 and 15:00–19:00 daily. Shops are open 09:00–13:00

and 15:00–18:00 Mon–Sat, some may close Sat afternoon; shops in resorts often stay open in the evenings in summer. Banking hours are 08:30–15:00 Mon–Fri. Most businesses are closed on public holidays.

Time Difference

Portugal is on GMT in winter and GMT +1 in summer (an hour earlier than Spain).

Communications

Post Offices open weekdays 08:30–18:00, larger branches also open Saturday mornings. Telephone calls can be made from metered phones in post offices, or from coin and card-operated call boxes. Buy phone cards in post offices, shops and cafés. Mobile phone coverage is excellent. For a local call you need to dial the area code, pre-fixed by a 2 rather than a 0. For example, if you are in Faro and calling a Faro number, you still have to dial 289.

Electricity

220 volts AC; standard European two pin plugs used.

Weights and Measures

The metric system is in use.

Health Precautions

Tap water is drinkable but bottled water is preferable. Mosquitoes can be a problem in summer; bring repellent. The sun is strong, so high factor pro-tection creams should be used and exposure limited at first.

Health Services

Most towns have a health centre (*centro de saúde*); state

CONVERSION CHART

FROM	TO	MULTIPLY BY
Millimetres	Inches	0.0394
Metres	Yards	1.0936
Metres	Feet	3.281
Kilometres	Miles	0.6214
Square kilometres	Square miles	0.386
Hectares	Acres	2.471
Litres	Pints	1.760
Kilograms	Pounds	2.205
Tonnes	Tons	0.984

To convert Celsius to Fahrenheit: x 9 ÷ 5 + 32

hospitals are located in Faro, tel: 289 891 100; Portimão, tel: 282 450 300; and Lagos, tel: 282 770 100. There are many English-speaking doctors and dentists in private practice in the Algarve; pharmacists can help you with minor ailments.

Personal Safety

The crime rate is quite low but petty theft is on the increase, and this is particularly true during summer months, when the Algarve is targeted by professional criminals looking for easy pickings from tourists. Keep bags and wallets secure when on the street and try to avoid carrying valuables. Bags and cameras should be locked away in the boot of the car.

Emergencies

In an emergency, dial **112** (no coins required) and ask the operator for police (*polícia*), fire services (*bombeiros*) or ambulance (*ambulância*). Many emergency services personnel do not speak English so try to enlist the aid of a local.

Etiquette

Courteous greetings and farewells (*bom dia, boa tarde, boa noite*), often accompanied by handshakes and kisses are part of the social fabric, but beyond this the Portuguese are quite informal. Good manners are the norm and are expected of visitors. In the Algarve locals are remarkably tolerant of the eccentricities of expats and tourists but rude, aggressive behaviour as well as excessive drinking is frowned upon.

Public Holidays and Festivals

Almost everything is closed and transport much reduced on holidays. Local holidays also affect opening times – check local papers for forthcoming events.

1 January •
New Year's Day
March/April •
(variable) Good Friday
25 April •
Revolution Day
1 May •
May Day
Early June •
(variable) Corpus Christi
10 June •
Camões Day
15 August •
Feast of the Assumption
5 October •
Republic Day
1 November •
All Saints Day
1 December •
National Independence Day
8 December •
Immaculate Conception
25 December •
Christmas Day

GOOD READING

Kaplan, Marion (2006) *The Portuguese*. Penguin.
Saramago, José, translated by Nick Caistor and Amanda Hopkinson (2002) *Journey to Portugal*. Harvill Press.
Anderson, Jean (1994) *The Food of Portugal*. William Morrow.
Birmingham, David (2003) *A Concise History of Portugal*. Cambridge.
Russell, Peter (2001) *Prince Henry the Navigator*. Yale Nota Bene.
Russell, AJR (1998) *The Portuguese Empire 1415–1808*. John Hopkins University.
Mayson, Richard (2003) *The Wines and Vineyards of Portugal*. Mitchell Beazley.
Vieira, Edite (2000) *The Taste of Portugal*. Grub Street.
Saraiva, José Hermano (1997) *Portugal: A Companion History*. Carcanet.

INDEX

accommodation 21, 38, 44–45, 47, 49, 50, 51, 52, 64–65, 71, 76, 82, 83, 97, 120–121, 122–126
Afonso III 13, 57, 95, 115
agriculture 12, 15, 20, **22**, 60, 61, 99, **93**, 100
Al Mutadid 55
Albufeira **19**, 27, 29, 44, **46**, 48–49, 50, 61
Alcantarilha 62
Alcoutim 85, 96
Aldeia da Tôr 43
Aldeia de Serra 118
Alentejo, The 5, 6, 8, 9, 11, 13, 31, 38, 96, 99–121
Algar Seco **53**
Algarve Tourist Board 122
Aljezur 81
Almancil 36, 39, 45
Almendres Stone Circle 108
Alte 25, 47, **59**
Alto Golf 28
Alvito 110
Alvor 68, 71
Anta do Zambujeio 108–109
Arade River 54, 56, 57, 58, 68, 69, 70
architecture 32–33, 36, 38, **41**, 42, 50, 53, 60, 61, 70, 75, 90, 91, 94, 103, 106, 116,
  Manueline 32, 58, 71, 80, 92, 103, 110, 112
  Pombaline 33
  see also Moors
Arco de Vila 36
Armação de Pêra 27, 44, 52, 53, 54
Avis Dynasty 16, 99, 105, 117
Ayamonte 94
azulejos **32**, 37, 39, 41, 58–60, 69, 73, 104, 106, 113

Barragem do Arade 58
Barrocal 7, 43
beaches 5, **6**, 27, 28, 35, 36, 38, 45, 47, 50, 53, 54, 63, 67, 70, 75, 78, **82**, 85, 87, 90, 94
  Albandeira 53
  Arrifana **82**
  Balaia 50
  Barranco 75
  Benagil 53
  Carvalho 53
  Centianes 53
  Dona Ana 75
  Falésia 27, 50
  Fishermen's Beach 48
  Ingrina 75

beaches (cont.)
  João Vaz 75
  Marinha 53
  Meia Praia 28
  Odeceixe 82
  Port Covo 82
  Praia da Bordeira 82
  Praia da Oura 49
  Praia da Rocha 9, 53, 67, **70**
  Praia de Beliche 78
  Praia de Pintadinho 54
  Praia do Amado 82
  Praia do Castelo 52, 82
  Praia do Martinhal 78
  Praia do Pinhão **6**
  Praia dos Barcos see Fishermen's Beach
  Praia dos Caneiros 54
  Praia dos Torrados 54
  Praia Grande 54
  Praia Senhora da Rocha 53
  Prainha 70
  Rio Sado 82
  São João de Arens 70
  sunbathing 78, 87
  Tonel 78
  Três Irmãos 70
  Vau 71
  Vila Nova de Milfontes 82
  Zaival 75
Beja 12, 33, 100–103, **104**
  Benagil 53
  Walk 54
birds 8, 38, 70, 77, 88, 89, 95
boat trips see cruises
Borba 117
Braganças 13, 16, 95, 99, 116, 117, 118
bullfighting **29**
Burgau 75
buses see transport

Cabanas 85, 92
Cabo de São Vicente 7, 11, **76**, **77**
Cachopo 92, 96
Caetano, Marcelo 18
Caldas de Monchique 79
camping 64–65, 76, 82, 83, 85, 97
Cape St Vincent
  see Cabo de São Vicente
Capote Alentejano 110, 111
cars 75, 97, 105, 120
  hire 124
  see also transport
caravel 14, 36, 78
Carlos I 13, 117
Carrapateira 82
Carthaginians 6, 12, 69, 76, 100
Carvoeiro 27, **54**, 64
Castro Marim 11, 85, 95
cataplana 52
chimney pots **96**

churches **81**, 110–111
  Albufeira
    São Sebastião 48
    Misericórdia Chapel 48
  Almansil
    São Lourenço 39
  Beja
    Nossa Senhora de Conceição Convent **103**
    Santa Amaro Church 103
    Santa Maria 103
  Estremoz
    São Francisco 113
    Santa Isabel 115
  Évora
    São Francisco **107**
  Faro
    Largo de São Francisco 37
  Lagos
    Santo António **73**
    Misericórdia 74
  Loulé
    São Francisco 41
    São Brás 41
    São Clemente **40**
  Monchique
    Convento da Nossa Senhora do Desterro 80
  Monsaraz
    Igreja Matriz de Santa Maria do Castelo 119
  Olhão
    Nossa Senhora do Rosário 87
    Nossa Senhora dos Aflitos **86**, 87
  Portimão
    Church of the Colégio 69
  Serpa
    Capela de São Gens **102**
    São Francisco Convent 101
  Tavira
    Church of the Misericórdia 91
    Santa Maria do Castelo 91
    Convento de Santo António **91**
    Igreja do Carmo 91
    Santo Sebastião 91
    São Francisco Monastery 91
  Vila Viçosa
    São Bartolomeu 116
    Nossa Senhora da Conceição 116
    Convento das Chagas 117
climate 5, 8, 9, 10, 35, 44, 45, 64, 83, 97, 100, 120
clubs see nightlife
coaches see transport
coffee 30
Columbus, Christopher 14, 76, 81

Compass Rose 15, **78**
conservation 7, 11, 67, 88–89, 92, 95
cork **8**, 10, 20, 56, 100, 109
Cromeleque dos Almendres 109
cruises 67, **68**, 75, 85, 87, 94, 96, 97
Crusades 13, 56, 58
culture 24–25, 59, 61
  dance **25**, 59
  music 24, 59, 102

Da Gama, Vasco 13, **15**
Dias, Bartolomeu 15
dolmens 108–111
  Olival de Pega 119
  Torre de Coelheiros **111**
  Zambujeiro **108**
Dom Afonso III 36, 61
Dom Dinis 13, 91, 102, 104, 112, 113, 115, 119
Dom Sebastião 15, 74
Drake, Francis 76, 78
Ducal Palace see Paço Ducal

Earthquake, The Great 13, 16, 17, 33, 36, 37, 48, 63, 90, 94, 95
economy 19–21
Estói 36, 42, 43, 45
  Palace **15**, 35, **42**, **43**
Estorninhos 93
Estremoz 8, 112, **113**, **114**, 115, 117, 119
etiquette 22, 126
European Community 13, 21
European Union 13, 19, 22
Évora 5, 6, 12, 19, 105–107, **112**, 119

farming 8, 12, 20, 61, 81, 93, 96, 99, 100, 102, 104, 118, 120
Faro 8, 9, 12, 15, 17, 19, 21, 29, 35–37, 42, 44–45, 48
Ferragudo 54
Ferreiras 44
ferry see transport
festivals 24, 25, 41, 57, 59, 103, 118, 126
Figueira 70
fishing 6, **20**, 31, 36, 48, 54, 68, 69, 71, 74, 75, 82, **87**, 88, 89, 90, **92**, 96, 97
flying 35, 44, 75, 123
Foia 7, 67, 79
Fonte de Benemola **7**, 43
food 30, **31**, 40, 45, 47, 62, 69, 71, 74, 80, 85, 86, 87, 92, 96, 106, 112, 113
football 29, 61
Foz da Odeleite 96

Galé 52, 53
Gilão River 90
Golden Coast 35
golf 5, 25–28, 38, 64
  courses **5**, 8, 25–28, 35,
  47, 50
government 7, 18, 19–21
Guadalupe 108
Guadiana River 7, 85, 94,
  96, 100, 102, 119
Guia 47, 62, 63
health 122, 125, 126
Henry the Navigator 13,
  14, 15, 70, 72, 74, 78
history 12–18, 69, 78, 93,
  99, 108–109, 119
holidays 126
horseriding 45, 65, 83, 96,
  97, 121
Horta da Moura 118, **119**, 121
hotels 28, 44, 96, 118
  see also accommodation
hunting 11, 88, 116
Ilha da Armona 85, 87, 97
Ilha da Culatra 85, 87
Ilha de Fuzeta 85
Ilha de Tavira 92
industry 6, 7, 17, 19, 20,
  21, 56, 87, 90, 96
Infante Dom Henrique
  see Henry the Navigator
Inquisition 16, 17, 105
Isabel 113, 115
islands 85, 87, 92

jeep safaris 96, 97
João I 14, 72, 105
João II 70, 86

Knights Templar 13, 85, 95

Lagoa 44, **60**
Lagos 5, 6, 14, 15, 17, 28,
  29, 44, 60, 67, 70, 72–74
land 5, 7–11, 21, 38, 67,
  68, 70, 79, 88, 99
language 23, 26, 109, 123
Largo Engo Duarte Pachero 49
latifúndios 12
legend 9, 57, 70, 72, 104, 116
Loulé 19, 35, 36, 40–41,
  44, 45, 96
  Gypsy Market 40, **41**, 59
Lusitano horses 29
Luz 75
Luz de Tavira 92

Manta Rota 85, 88, 92
Marialva, Marquês de 42
markets **31**, 40, 43, 69, 74, 80
Martim Longo 96
menhirs 108, 109, 119
Mértola 12, 96, 100–101, 119
Mesquita 101
Messines see São
  Bartolomeu de Messines

Milreu **12**, 42
Mina de São Domingo 102
Miradouro de Caldeirão 43
Monchique 44, 67,70,
  79, **80**, 81
Monsaraz 118, 119
Monte dos Almendres 109
Monte Gordo 85, 94
Montechoro 44, 49
Moors 6, 7, 9, 12, 13, 29,
  33, 35, 36, 37, 38, 40, 43,
  48, 55, 56, 57, 58, 61, 62,
  68, 70, 71, 75, 79, 81, 90,
  91, 99, 100, 102, 103,
  119, see also architecture
mountains 7, 67, 79
museums 33, 80, 101, 102
  Beja
    Convento da Nossa
    Senhora da Conceição
    33
  Estremoz
    Museu Rural 113
    Railway Museum 14
    Municipal Museum 115
  Évora
    Museum of Sacred Art 106
  Lagos
    Museum of the Great
    Discoveries 33, 72
    Municipal Museum 73
  Silves
    Archaeology Museum
    33, 58
  Vila Viçosa
    Museum of Hunting
    116

navigators 14, 15, 78
nightlife 47, 49, 91
nora **9**
Nossa Senhora de
  Conceição Convent **103**
Olaria Pequena 62

Olhão 85, 86–87

Paço Ducal 116
Paderne 47, **61**
Parque da Floresta 28
passports 122
Penedo Gordo 104
Penina 28
people 22–33
  culture 22, 24–25
  dress 22, 110
  festivals 24, 25
Phoenicians 6, 13, 55, 68,
  76, 96, 100
Pine Cliffs 27
  Golf and Country Club 50
Pinheiros Altos 26, 35, 38,
plant life 7, 8, 9, 10, 43, 77,
  79, 81, 93, 99
Pombal, Marquês de 16, **17**,
  74, 94

Ponte da Piedade 75
population 7, 20, 21, 48, 59
Porches 62
Portel 111
Portimão **16**, 29, 60, 67–71
Porto Santo 15
post offices 125
pottery **21**, 40, 62, 119
pousada 110, **111**, 115,
  117, 120–121

Quarteira 29, 51
Quarteira River 61
Querença 43
Quinta do Gramacho 27
Quinta do Lago 25, **26**,
  30, 35, 36, 38, 45, 88

Redondo **118**, 119
religion 16, 23, 24, 42, 72,
  87, 95, 103, 109
Reserva do Sapal 95
resorts 21, 38, 47, 48, 50,
  52, 67, 70, 75, 85, 92, 94
restaurants 37, 38, 39, 45,
  48, 62, 65, 71, 74, 83,
  91, 97, 121, 124
revolution 18, 20, 61,
  104
Ria Formosa Nature Reserve
  11, 25, 36, 38, 85, **88**, 89
rock formations **66**, 70
Romans 6, 12, 13, 35, 42,
  48, 50, 61, 68, 70, 76,
  89, 90, 99, 100, 104,
  105, 109, 110, 111, 119

safaris 75
Sagres 15, 47, 67, 76, 78
Salazar, Dr António 13, 18,
  20, 21, 42, 61, 103
Salema 28, **75**
Salgados 27
Salir 43
San Lorenzo 25, 35, 38
Sanlucar de Guadiana 96
Santa Catarina 70
Santa Luzia 92
São Bartolomeu de Messines
  58
São Brás de Alportel 42
São Manços 118
São Pedro do Corval 119
São Rafael **53**
Second Punic war 12
Senhora da Rocha 54
Serpa 100, **102**
Serra d'Ossa 8, 118
Serra de Alcaria do Cume
  92
Serra de Monchique 55, 79, **98**
Serra do Caldeirão 35, 36,
  42
Sheraton Hotel 27, 50
shopping 37, 38, 40, 49, 69,
  74, 79, 96, 119, 125

Silves 5, 12, 33, 44, 47, **55**,
  56, **57**, **58**, 68, 69
snooker 29
Soares, Mario 19
Sotavento 85
Spanish War 103
sport 5, 9, 25, 29, 35, 38, 39,
  44, 45, 50, 52, 64, 65, 70,
  71, 75, 82, 83, 97, 121, 74
  see also golf courses
stone circles 108, **109**, 119
storks **11**, 36, 90

Tavira 7, 17, 60, **84**, 90–93
taxis see transport
telephones 125, 126
Temple of Diana **105**
Torre de Coelheiros 109
tours 45, 65, 75, 83, 97, 121
  operators 45, 83, 97, 121
tourism 6, 19, 21, 47, 48,
  75, 76, 96, 121
tourist offices 45, 65, 69, 83,
  90, 97, 113, 119, 121,
  122
transport 122, 124–125
  buses 44, 64, 83, 90, 97,
  120, 123, 125
  coaches 83, 97, 123
  ferry 90, 94, 97
  taxis 44, 123, 125
  trains 44, 64, 83, 97,
  120, 123
travel 122–126
Tumulos de Alcalar 70

Vale da Pinta 27
Vale de Milho 27
Vale do Lobo 26, **27**, **28**,
  30, 35, 36, 38–39, 45
Vaqueiros 96
Vascão River 100
vegetation 7, 8, 9, 10, 77
Viana do Alentejo **110**
Vila Abicada 70
Vila do Infante 76, 78
Vila Real de Santo António
  9, 29, 47, 85, **94**, **95**,
  100
Vila Sol 26
Vila Viçosa 99, **116**, **117**
Vilamoura 26, 27, **50**, 51
Visigoths 12, 13, 42, 50, 99,
  119

War of Succession 102
War of the Two Brothers
  13, 17, 48, 112
Water Dog **89**
Water Parks 47, 51, **63**
wetlands 8, 88
wildlife 7, 10, 11, 77, 88
wine 6, 15, **31**, 60, 80, 94,
  100, 118, 119

Zoomarine 63